# Folding Stories

## Storytelling and Origami Together As One

by Christine Petrell Kallevig

photographs by Eleanor Draper

INTERNATIONAL

P. O. Box 813, Newburgh, Indiana 47629

Storytime Ink International
P. O. Box 813, Newburgh, IN 47629

ISBN 0-9628769-0-9

Illustrations by Christine Petrell Kallevig.

First Edition
10 9 8 7 6 5 4 3 2 1
Printed in the United States of America

Library of Congress Catalog Card Number: 91-90852

ACKNOWLEDGMENTS
Procedure for folding the bunny was learned from Samuel Randlett in *The Art Of
Origami*, (E. P. Dutton & Co., Inc. 1961), p. 35.

Procedure for folding the bird was learned from Isao Honda in *The World Of
Origami*, (Japan Publication Trading Co., 1965), p. 44.

Procedure for folding the fish was learned from Ian Adair in *Papercrafts*, (David &
Charles Publishers, 1975).

Procedure for folding the traditional sea bream was learned from Toyoaki Kawai in
*Japan's Creative Origami*, (Ottenheimer Publishers, 1988), p. 60.

Procedure for folding the magic square was learned from Kazuo Kobayashi and
Makoto Yamaguchi in *Origami for Parties*, (Kodansha International LTD. 1987),
p. 28.

*The author expresses appreciation to...*

Lillian Oppenheimer, the founder of the Origami Center of America, for her gracious encouragement and words of support.

Nancy Schimmel, the wonderful California storyteller, for her insight and valuable ideas in plotting and design.

Anne Pellowski, the founder of the Information Center on Children's Cultures of the U. S. Committee for UNICEF, for her storytelling suggestions.

Dr. Diane Doepker Holihan, an award winning educator and valued friend, for her astute editing and careful proof-reading.

Andrea Brown, a respected journalist and friend, for her suggestions regarding character and plot development.

Barbara Hendricks, for her limitless enthusiasm and support.

Eleanor Draper, for her creative and sensitive photography skills.

Bob Etheridge of Micro Computer Systems, Inc. for his technological assistance.

Jim, David, and Paul Kallevig for their help, patience, and support.

o the ancient paper folders and storytellers who created art forms that are eternally fascinating, always evolving, and forever descriptive of the essence of the human spirit.

TABLE OF CONTENTS

# Why combine storytelling and paper folding?

Storytelling and origami (Japanese *ori* meaning "folded" and *kami* or *gami* meaning "paper") are both ancient arts deeply embedded in family oral tradition. Virtually every culture in the world employs storytelling techniques to preserve traditions, establish moral values, entertain, or communicate information and feelings. Although exact dates are unknown, most scholars believe that Japanese paper folding was first practiced in the 6th century A. D. when Buddhist monks carried paper to Japan from China. Paper was expensive and precious in the early centuries, so paper folding techniques were practiced and preserved by religious leaders. Later, as paper became readily available, origami traditions were passed down through the generations by Japanese mothers. Origami became in important aspect of every Japanese child's education.

Paper folding techniques were also developed or reinvented in Europe, perhaps as a natural extension of cloth folding. Leonardo da Vinci used folding in his illustrations and the *XI Book of Euclid* used folding to demonstrate geometric designs. Early German architects emphasized paper folding in testing basic engineering principles.

In contrast, most modern Americans view paper folding as a craft or hobby. Americans are usually first introduced to paper folding at school or on the playground in the construction of paper hats, airplanes, or "cootie-catchers" (also called "fortune-tellers"). Some of us disguised Junior High notes by folding them into boxes or triangles. Perhaps we designed paper boats or homemade envelopes. Although gaining in popularity, the often intricate models found in Japanese paper folding techniques are not usually included in typical American educational experiences.

I was first introduced to origami at a museum workshop. Several parents and their children were gathered around a single origami artist who was demonstrating how to fold a traditional flapping crane. Like the other spectators, I was both intrigued and frustrated. Although I have always considered myself to be "artsy-craftsy" and comfortable with intricate handwork, I could not follow along or remember the sequence of steps necessary to build the model.

Some of the children had lost interest and were no longer focused on the artist. They were noisy and running around, making it difficult to concentrate. Paper folding was also too new to me. I didn't understand "mountain" or "valley" folding, or the other terms the artist used. I couldn't relate the steps to anything in my personal background. I finally gave up trying to fold along, and instead, watched as the figure took shape. The techniques of converting a flat piece of paper into a three dimensional object were amazing then and continue to fascinate me.

Even more exciting, however, was the idea that came to me as I watched the crane emerge... if the artist would tell a story as he folded the crane, I believed that I could learn and remember the sequence of folds more effectively. I would have something to relate the folds to, something concrete to remember. Groups, even as diverse as the one I was a part of, would be united by the structure of the story. The story would maintain the attention of even the youngest folders. I immediately saw the educational benefits of this concept: memory enhancement, fine-motor coordination, right/left brain interaction, and an effective way to teach an art form whose only financial investment was a piece of paper.

Needless to say, I rushed home with more energy and enthusiasm than anyone else at that workshop! Storigami was born!

## What is Storigami?

The concept is simple. Storytelling + Origami = Storigami. In other words, create a delightful story, then illustrate the events of the story with actual origami folds. When the story is ended, the simple three dimensional model is complete. Recalling the sequence of events in the story is the same as recalling the sequence of folds necessary to make the origami figure.

After developing this concept for over a year, I discovered that there were some other authors who had also been excited by the same idea. Like the origami models themselves, the Storigami concept is no doubt a technique that has been invented and reinvented over and over throughout history. Good ideas are rarely actually *new* ideas. New applications of good ideas, however, are cause for celebration!

Those interested in other work that combines origami and text, will find references in the "For more information" section on page 85 of this book.

## Is previous storytelling or origami experience required?

No! The strength of this system is its simplicity. There are no complicated symbols or specialized terms in the directions. The illustrations were drawn so that beginners with no previous origami experience can fold with

success and confidence. Optional introductory statements are offered for storytellers who stumble over the "getting started" phase.

But please read the next section called, "Before you begin." It is loaded with tips based on experiences gained from the field-testing phase of this book.

## Who should practice Storigami?

**Art teachers** who would like to introduce origami in an entertaining and non-threatening way to inexperienced paper folders.

**Children's librarians** who would like to combine an inexpensive paper craft with literature that American children will both enjoy and identify.

**Storytellers** who enjoy new and unusual props to peak their listeners' interest.

**Activity therapists** who are challenged by groups composed of individuals with diverse interests and levels of sophistication.

**Recreation, troop and club leaders** who organize and present wholesome activities on limited budgets.

**Origami specialists** who present workshops to novice folders and would like to introduce basic folding techniques in an interesting and unusual format.

**Parents, grandparents, uncles & aunts** who would like to spice up family activities with a fun and inexpensive new hobby.

**Teachers** seeking to supplement basic subject matter in a shared learning experience for students with diverse learning styles, abilities and cultural experiences.

**For best results,
follow these guidelines:**

1. Match the story to your group.

2. Pre-fold the origami figure.

3. Have required materials prepared.

4. Be familiar with the story.

5. Enhance the story with related activities.

6. Plan a response to reluctant folders.

7. Expect and accept imperfect first folds.

8. Understand folding directions.

## Match the story to your group.

Every story in this book features a different origami model. All of the stories can be enjoyed on a superficial, literal level by young children or may be interpreted on deeper levels by older, more sophisticated audiences. All of the origami figures were selected because they are among the easiest and least complex models to make. Success with these simple models help non-folders feel confident and comfortable with elementary paper-folding techniques. However, even with these basic models, varying levels of difficulty exist. It is important to select stories that match your group's abilities, ages, interests, and developmental levels.

It is perfectly acceptable to tell the stories without teaching the folds, particularly if you have time constraints or your group size is too large or too young to learn the folds effectively.

## Pre-fold the origami figure for most effective storytelling.

The most pleasing origami models are constructed with clean, sharp folds where the paper edges are precisely aligned. Expert folders can accomplish this feat without the support of a hard, flat surface. But the rest of us need a flat surface to make accurate creases. Unfortunately, hard flat surfaces are not always available or practical in storytelling locations.

To overcome this presentation problem and to be able to tell the story smoothly without taking excessive folding time, it is *essential* to pre-fold the model featured in your selected story. Then, as you approach each step, the folds will simply snap into place. You will not fumble with the paper nor suddenly forget what to do. Your story delivery will be confident and dynamic as you concentrate on the story text and your group's responses.

## Have all required materials ready before you begin.

The title page for each story includes a photograph of the featured origami model, a brief description of the story, and a list of materials required for the presentation of the story. If you plan to teach the model or use the story to support other activities, you will need several squares of paper for each group member. Plan to have plenty of paper for practice or mistakes.

## Be familiar with the text.

Experienced storytellers will want to memorize the stories for their presentations. But others will want to refer to the book as they present the stories. For this reason, the photos of the featured origami figures are placed on the title pages *only*, so that when the story is open in front of a group, the listeners will not be able to see what figure will finally emerge.

This element of surprise makes the stories more intriguing and ironic. Listeners of all ages are delighted when the final figure emerges. As always, story presentations are most effective when the storyteller is very familiar with the material.

## Enhance the stories with optional activities.

All of the stories include suggestions for additional optional activities. The index refers to subjects addressed in the stories themselves or in these activity options.

The stories fit neatly into a wide variety of subject areas or units of study. Many of the optional activities have been labeled according to particular memory or thinking skills for the convenience of those interested in promoting these abilities.

Not all of the activities are appropriate for all groups and are not designed to be presented together. They are merely suggestions for the storyteller or are intended to spark a new idea for a creative application. Areas have been designated in these sections for logging your own applications or making notes about the response of your group to the activities you tried. It is often helpful to note presentation details so that future planning can be facilitated.

## Plan a response for reluctant folders.

Some children and adults are so afraid of ruining the paper, making mistakes or attempting new activities that they won't even try. They exclaim loudly, "I *can't* do it!"

One way to overcome this reluctance is to avoid distributing practice paper until the story is finished and the folding sequence has been reviewed. This helps the group feel confident about remembering what comes next and eliminates worry related to forgetfulness.

Discourage participants from folding along as you first tell the story. This distracts other group members and reduces the folder's ability to associate the story events with the progressive folding steps. Learning would therefore be less effective.

Another successful technique is to fold each step together as a group, saying often, "Yes! That's right. This is easy." Affirming that the task is not hard and publicly complimenting successful efforts sets a positive tone for beginners.

A third method of reassuring reluctant folders is for the storyteller to do something silly or clumsy: drop paper, forget someone's name, start over because of an uneven crease, etc. *It is important that the storyteller never confuse the group by mixing up the folds,* but silly little errors often puts an anxious group at ease. Too much perfection or seriousness promotes folding reluctance. The stories are whimsical and should be presented with a light-hearted tone.

## Expect and accept imperfect folds from beginners.

New paper folders sometimes feel overwhelmed by the experience. During the first folding trial, concentrate on following the sequence of steps necessary to create the model. Most beginners are pleased with their results and surprised that paper folding really is easy. They immediately want to make another one.

During second and third attempts, begin to emphasize the quality and sharpness of the folds, suggesting that the model will be more attractive when all of the edges and corners are lined up exactly during every step.

Avoid criticizing lop-sided or ragged first results. Instead, say, "Yes! I *knew* you could do it! Let's make another one to share. This time, try lining up the edges before you crease the paper. That might help it stand up better."

9

# How to make the origami figures:

1.  Every story includes a summary of folding directions. Use these directions when pre-folding the origami figure. Then go back to see where the folds occur in the story. Always use a pre-folded model to tell the stories. (Simply unfold the completed model so that all the necessary creases will already be there.)

2.  All figures in this book start as squares. It is important that the squares be exactly the same length on all sides.

3.  Origami paper can be purchased pre-cut in a variety of beautiful colors and textures. However, all of the figures in this book can be made very successfully with paper you already have in your home, office or classroom. Experiment with different weights and textures for the most satisfying results.

4.  Use a hard, flat surface when making initial folds. Line up edges and corners precisely and hold in place before you crease.

5.  Follow each step in the directions in the order they are given. Only after you are very proficient in making a figure, should you attempt to alter the established technique.

6.  Explanation of symbols:

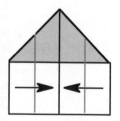

Shaded areas indicate that the back side of the paper is now facing up.

Arrows point to the direction of the fold.

Dotted or dashed lines mark where the next crease will be.

Solid lines indicate existing creases, folds, or edges.

This simple bird is constructed in six steps. Folding directions begin on page 16.

F
O
R

E
A
C
H

A

H
A
T

**About the story:**

Mattie Matter the Hatter tries to find perfect hats for her customers and perfect customers for her hats. She is usually successful, but sometimes unexpected things happen...

**Recommended ages:**

Listening only:  age 3 through adult.
Listening and folding:  age 5 through adult.

**Required materials:**

1 square of paper at least 6 inches each side, folded into a bird and then completely unfolded for storytelling.

**Optional introductory statement:**

*I'm going to tell you a story about something very strange that happened to a hat maker named Mattie Matter the Hatter. As I tell you the story, watch very carefully as I fold paper into various shapes. This is called origami, or Japanese paper folding. Do you have any questions? (pause) The name of the story is "For Each A Hat".*

# For Each, A Hat....

Mattie Matter the Hatter believes that for every person there is the perfect hat, and for every hat, there is the perfect person. The trouble is, most people don't know which hats are just right for them and they end up walking around with mismatched, unhappy hats on their heads. Mattie Matter the Hatter knows hats better than she knows anything else in the world, and she believes that hats know exactly which people they should belong to.

But hats are secretive. They don't just jump off the shelf onto an unsuspecting person's head. A hat relies on its distinct personality to attract a proper owner. The happiest hats have personalities that match their owner's exactly.

Mattie Matter the Hatter tells her customers that a sure way of knowing that your hat is happy with you is that you are able to find it after a year or so. If your hat is unhappy, it will get lost in a closet, blow away in the wind, arrange to get sat on, or go home with someone else. Some mismatched hats go to extreme measures to get away from the wrong people, but most often, they simply disappear.

One day a very quiet young woman tiptoed into Mattie Matter the Hatter's Hat Shop. She glided silently over to the triangular hats, selected a plain one like this *(hold fold #1 above your eyebrows as though it was a triangular hat)* and slid it down over her eyes.

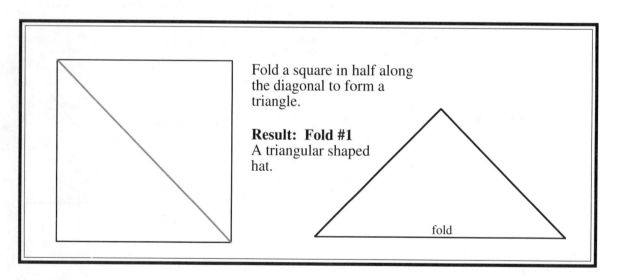

Fold a square in half along the diagonal to form a triangle.

**Result: Fold #1**
A triangular shaped hat.

fold

A slight smile graced her lips as she whispered, "This is the hat for me."

And it was.

Another day, a blushing freckle faced boy carrying a fishing rod rushed in and darted from shelf to shelf until his eyes lit upon this wide brimmed straw hat *(hold up fold #2)*:

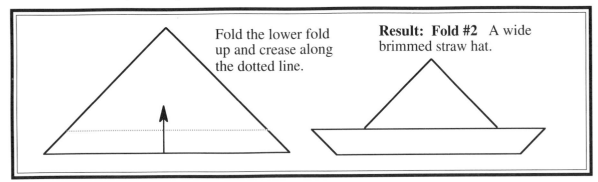

"My mom says that I have to wear a hat to keep out the sun or she won't let me go fishin' today. What do you think of this one?"

"Just right!" said Mattie Matter the Hatter.

And it was!

Five minutes later, a taller blushing freckle faced boy carrying a fishing rod rushed into the shop. "I need a fishing hat just like my little brother's, but I don't want to get it mixed up with his....."

"No problem," said Mattie Matter the Hatter. She took another fishing hat off the shelf and turned it over like this *(flip the fold to the other side)* and pulled the top down like this *(hold up fold #3 as shown)*:

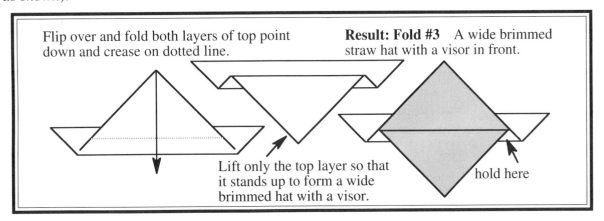

"Now you have a visor on your hat," she told the boy.

"Will it bring me good luck fishin' today?" asked the boy.

"I believe it will," said Mattie Matter the Hatter.

And it did!

Another day there was a boom of thunder and a sudden unexpected downpour of rain caught everyone without their umbrellas. A flustered woman with wet newspaper clumped on top of her very curly, stinky hair huffed through the door.

"My new hairdo will be ruined in the rain! I have to go home right away! Please help me!" she pleaded as she picked gobs of wet newspaper out of her stinky curls.

"No problem," said Mattie Matter the Hatter. She took a visor fishing hat off the shelf and folded it in half like this *(demonstrate with fold #4 as shown)*:

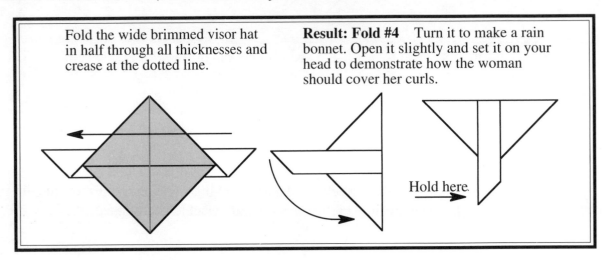

Fold the wide brimmed visor hat in half through all thicknesses and crease at the dotted line.

**Result: Fold #4**   Turn it to make a rain bonnet. Open it slightly and set it on your head to demonstrate how the woman should cover her curls.

Hold here

"Don't worry about the rain, dear. Just cover your curls with this rain bonnet."

"Oh thank you, thank you, thank you! This is exactly what I need to get my new hairdo home safely!" exclaimed the woman.

And it was!

After it stopped raining that day, the clouds did not lighten as usual, but stayed very dark and gloomy. "I don't like the looks of the sky," said Mattie Matter the Hatter. "I think I'll close the shop and go home."

Just as she was about to lock the front door, a gnarled green hand with thick yellow claws gripped the door and shoved it open. The longest, greenest and crookedest nose that Mattie Matter the Hatter had ever seen poked around the doorway. Narrow red eyes could scarcely be seen under its tangled purple hair. The creature was dressed in black rags and carried an old jagged broomstick.

"I need a new hat," hissed the witch.

Mattie Matter the Hatter could not think of one hat in her shop that would want to go home with a witch. But she always tried to please her customers, no matter who they were.

"Perhaps this rain bonnet would do," she suggested. "I've already sold a dozen of them this afternoon and it looks like we might be in for more rain. You could hook it under that very sharp chin of yours."

"No!" hissed the witch. Her harsh voice sent a fearful tremor through the hat shop. "I need a pointed, crooked hat to match my pointed, crooked nose!"

"Yes, it is quite crooked," agreed Mattie Matter the Hatter. "Perhaps you could simply hook the rain bonnet to it..."

"No!" hissed the witch.

"Well, all right....let me see what I can make for you. I must warn you, though. Some of my hats are rather stubborn. If they don't feel right with you, they will find a way to leave you."

"I know!" screeched the witch. "What do you think happened to my other hats? I've never been able to keep a hat for more than a day!"

"I believe I can make you a crooked hat, but it doesn't come with a money back guarantee. Once you leave the shop, you're on your own."

Mattie Matter the Hatter folded up the straps of the rain bonnet on both sides like this *(fold #5 as shown)* and made the witch a pointed, crooked hat to match her pointed, crooked nose.

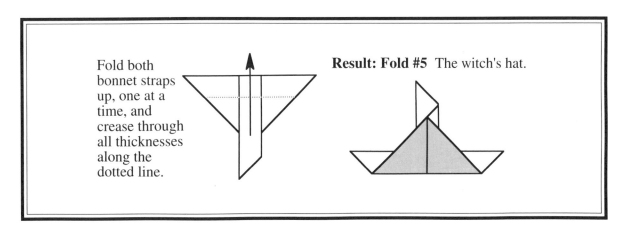

Fold both bonnet straps up, one at a time, and crease through all thicknesses along the dotted line.

**Result: Fold #5** The witch's hat.

The witch snatched it with her yellow claws and crammed it over her wild purple hair. "This looks just right," she hissed as she sat on her broom and zoomed away through the door.

But it wasn't just right......

Just as the witch flew above the shop and was about to vanish into one of the mysteriously dark clouds, the most amazing thing happened. The hat sprouted wings and a beak like this *(fold #6 as shown)* and flew all the way back to the roof of Mattie Matter the Hatter's Hat Shop.

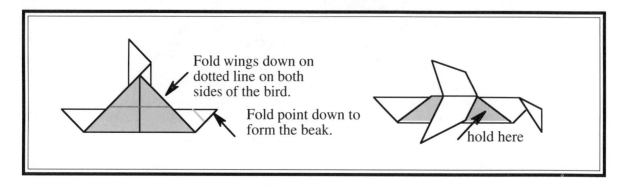

Fold wings down on dotted line on both sides of the bird.

Fold point down to form the beak.

hold here

The hat-bird stayed on the roof for about a week, examining all the people walking by on the sidewalk below. It must have spotted just the right person to go home with, for suddenly it disappeared and never came back again.

Yes, for every person there is the perfect hat, and for every hat, the perfect person.

# Summary of folding directions:

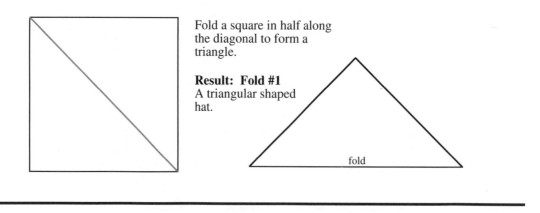

Fold a square in half along the diagonal to form a triangle.

**Result: Fold #1**
A triangular shaped hat.

fold

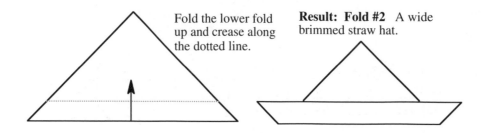

Fold the lower fold up and crease along the dotted line.

**Result: Fold #2** A wide brimmed straw hat.

Flip over and fold both layers of top point down and crease on dotted line.

**Result: Fold #3**  A wide brimmed straw hat with a visor in front.

Lift only the top layer so that it stands up to form a wide brimmed hat with a visor.

hold here

Fold the wide brimmed visor hat in half through all thicknesses and crease at the dotted line.

**Result: Fold #4**  Turn it to make a rain bonnet. Open it slightly and set it on your head to demonstrate how the woman should cover her curls.

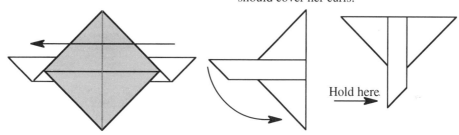

Hold here.

Fold both bonnet straps up, one at a time, and crease through all thicknesses along the dotted line.

**Result: Fold #5**  The witch's hat.

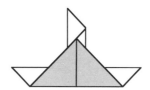

Fold wings down on dotted line on both sides of the bird.

Fold point down to form the beak.

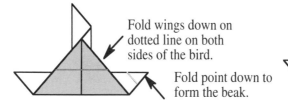

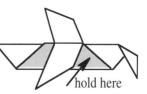

hold here

# Optional applications for "For Each, A Hat..."

1. After telling the story, ask the listeners to identify the different characters in the order they were introduced *(auditory memory)*. Then ask them to name the characters' hat preferences in the same order *(visual memory)*. Construct the bird again, letting the group tell you which "hat" comes next. Then distribute squares of paper and fold each "hat" together as a group *(synthesis)*.

2. It is often interesting to decorate the finished model and then completely unfold it to see where the decorative marks are on the original square of paper. Fold it into the final form again and watch the decorations reappear in their intended places *(analysis)*. Before unfolding, ask where they think the decorative marks will be on the flat paper *(evaluation)*.

3. Make a mobile with all the birds or tape them to a branch with many twigs. Emphasize unity, friendship and a sense of belonging within the group. Say, "We all made this together...."

4. Decorate a table with a birdfeeder for the birds and serve nuts and sunflower seeds (or items made from these things) as a snack.

5. Use the story to lead into discussions or units on:
   a. Birds.
   b. Losing things. Do we lose things we don't like? Can things really get lost on purpose?
   c. Belonging. How do you know when things (people) truly belong together?
   d. Hats.
   e. Shyness (the quiet young lady).
   f. Excitement (the eager young fishermen).
   g. Anxiety (the woman worried about her hair).
   h. Hostility (the witch).
   i. Satisfaction (the bird finally finding its proper owner).
   j. The many different hats (roles) that people play.

6. Divide into teams for silly birdbrain relays and contests.

7. Customize the birds by adding extra folds on the tail, head, beak and wings. Change the shape of the body by widening the "brim" on fold #2 *(synthesis)*.

8. Study different bird families and identify the reasons why beaks are different shapes *(analysis)*. Mold the beaks of the paper birds into these various shapes *(synthesis)*.

| Date | Group | Notes |
|---|---|---|
|  |  |  |
|  |  |  |
|  |  |  |
|  |  |  |
|  |  |  |

This traditional helmet is made in seven simple steps. Folding directions begin on page 24.

**About the story:**

Have you ever wondered why donkeys say "Hee-Haw"? This story gives an improbable, but entertaining explanation.

**Recommended ages:**

Listening only:  ages 3 through adult.
Listening and folding:  age 5 through adult.

**Required materials:**

1 square of paper at least 6 inches each side, folded into a hat and then completely unfolded for storytelling. Note: a 7" square yields a 5" hat. To make a hat large enough to wear, use a 22" square of newspaper.

**Optional introductory statement:**

*I'm going to tell you a story about why donkeys began to say "Hee-Haw". As I tell you the story, watch very carefully as I fold paper into various shapes. This is called origami, or Japanese paper folding. Do you have any questions? (pause) The name of the story is "How The Donkey Got His Haw".*

# How The Donkey Got His Haw

Long ago after the giant dinosaurs disappeared from the Earth and before there were very many people around, animals freely wandered over the land. There were no fences or highways or cities to block their way. Donkeys were especially common, but they were quite a bit different than the donkeys we see today.

Modern donkeys have long ears that stand straight up, but old-fashioned donkeys had long ears that drooped down over their faces like this *(show fold #1 and #2 as follows)*:

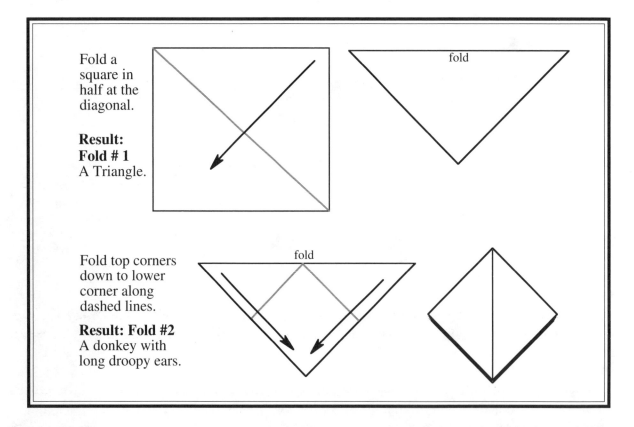

When donkeys lowered their heads to tear out a mouthful of fresh spring clover, their ears would sway and wag like this *(move the tips of the fold back and forth)*. Whenever the donkeys tried to look around, their long floppy ears would cover their eyes *(fold the tips down to the center point again)*. This was handy when they wanted to take a nap during the day, but most of the time, having long drooping ears was very inconvenient. They could hardly see beyond the tips of their ears.

In the old days, donkeys were best friends with the brown sparrows who followed them from meadow to meadow. The light-hearted birds sat together in the shade trees surrounding the plush grazing lands. They twittered and tweeted all day long about the funny things they had seen or heard on their travels with the donkeys. Each bird competed to sing the most amusing song, or to tell the most interesting bit of news. Their droopy-eared donkey friends were the judges. If a sparrow's story or song could make a donkey stop munching for a minute and throw back his head with a jolly, "Hee Hee! Hee Hee!", then it was a winner. The sparrows loved to hear the donkeys laugh, so they grew sillier and more entertaining every day.

One sunny afternoon, the brown sparrows were gathered in the top branches of a lone elm tree. They had a perfect view of the meadow all around them. An old-fashioned, droopy-eared donkey was munching grass in the shade of their tree, and a family of baby piglets was mucking about in the puddles next to a hillside dotted with the blooms of wild daisies. Every now and then, the donkey forgot himself and lifted his nose up beyond his ears, blurting out a joyous, "Hee Hee! Hee Hee!"

But then one of the sparrows said, "Look - it! Look - it! The pigs! Roll - ing! Roll - ing! Tweet-tut! Tweet-tut!"

(That was sparrow talk for, "Isn't that hilarious?")

Nodding and tossing his head back and forth as fast as he could, *(do the same with the tips of the fold)* the donkey could not keep his ears away from his eyes long enough to watch the pigs. When the donkey threw his head this way, one ear would cover his eyes like this *(demonstrate with the fold)* and when he tossed his head that way, the other ear would cover his eyes like this *(demonstrate with the fold)*. Soon the sparrows stopped laughing at the pigs rolling about and instead, they began to laugh at the donkey whipping his ears all around.

"Don - Key! Don - Key! Tweet-tut! Tweet-tut!"

The sparrows all had a good long laugh. So long, in fact, that the donkey shamefully lowered his head so that his ears covered his whole face *(fold the corners back to the center to close up the fold)*.

The sparrows hadn't meant to hurt his feelings. To cheer him up, they decided to take turns holding up his ears. One sparrow dipped down out of the elm tree, snatched up the bottom point of the donkey's ear and flew in place above his head. Another sparrow held the other ear. *(Demonstrate by holding the fold by the tips of the lower points. It will fall open into the large triangle again)*.

The donkey was so excited that he brayed with joy. "Hee Hee! Hee Hee! I see!"

All the sparrows took a turn at holding up the donkey's ears, but they soon grew exhausted from having to fly in place for so long. When they simply could not hold his ears any more, the donkey lowered his head with even deeper disappointment than before.

The donkey felt so sad about his floppy-ear problem that he refused to laugh at the sparrows' jokes. The birds couldn't compete for the day's funniest story when they no longer had a judge. So they decided to invent a new way to hold up the donkey's ears. Two sparrows folded up the donkey's ears like this, one on each side *(fold #3 as shown)*:

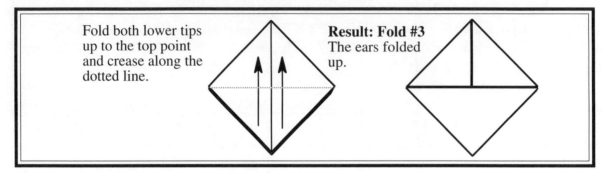

Fold both lower tips up to the top point and crease along the dotted line.

**Result: Fold #3**
The ears folded up.

Two other birds gathered straw to make a headband to pin the ears up like this *(fold #4 as shown)*:

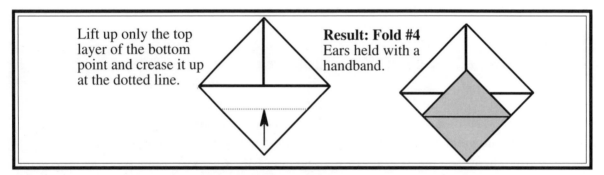

Lift up only the top layer of the bottom point and crease it up at the dotted line.

**Result: Fold #4**
Ears held with a handband.

But the floppy ears just wouldn't stay in place *(demonstrate by letting the top points pop out of place)*. The birds decided to tighten the donkey's new headband by folding its lower edge up like this *(fold #5 as shown)*:

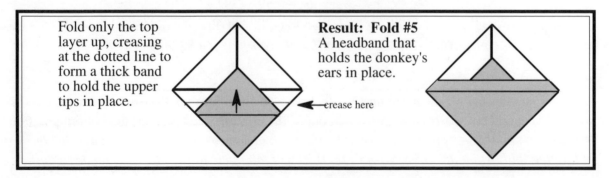

Fold only the top layer up, creasing at the dotted line to form a thick band to hold the upper tips in place.

crease here

**Result: Fold #5**
A headband that holds the donkey's ears in place.

This new headband fit the donkey's head very nicely, so the birds expanded it to make a simple little hat *(slip your fingers into the fold to show how it fit on his head)*. It was working perfectly to keep the donkey's ears out of his eyes, but it kept falling off because the back part of it hung down too low on the donkey's mane *(point out the back flap of the fold)*. The sparrows were tired of always having to pick it up off the ground and put it back on, so they decided to just get the back flap out of the way by tucking it into the hat like this *(fold #6 as shown):*

"Hee Hee! Hee Hee! I see!" shouted the donkey. Thanks to the sparrows' wonderful invention, he was happy to be a storytelling judge again.

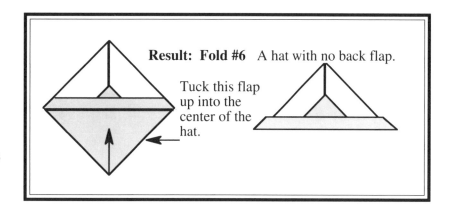

**Result: Fold #6** A hat with no back flap.

Tuck this flap up into the center of the hat.

With all this good fortune, you'd expect that the sparrows and the donkey would go right back to their usual cheerful afternoons together. But with the donkey's ears folded so tightly into his new hat, the donkey couldn't hear very well. He had to strain to hear the sparrows clearly. This new problem made him grumpy and short-tempered. When he couldn't hear a complete story, he would shout, "Haw? Haw? Haw? Haw?"

After a few frustrating weeks, the sparrows lost their judge again when the donkey refused to even try to listen. The only sounds he ever made were rude blasts of, "Haw? Haw? Haw? Haw?"

With no patience left, an irritated sparrow dipped down from the tree to snatch the hat right off his head. After all, a jolly donkey who couldn't see was better than a grouchy one that couldn't hear. But the hat had been on the donkey's head for so long, that it wouldn't come off. The bird did split open a hole, however, and pop! Out sprang one of the donkey's ears like this *(fold #7 as shown).* Another bird tore a hole in the other side as well.

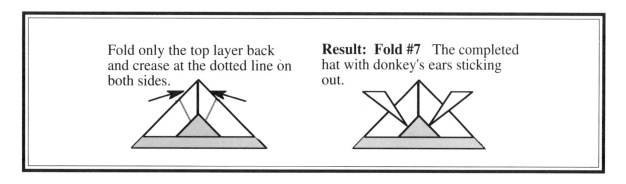

Fold only the top layer back and crease at the dotted line on both sides.

**Result: Fold #7** The completed hat with donkey's ears sticking out.

Now the donkey could see and hear! He was thrilled, but after weeks of shouting "Haw? Haw?" all the time, he had forgotten how to be happy! So he threw back his head and let a new laugh come bubbling out.

"Hee Haw! Hee Haw!"

The donkey and his inventive sparrow friends liked the sound of his new laugh so well that donkeys still laugh the same way today. Over the years, the hats helped donkey ears grow tall and straight until, finally, donkeys didn't need them any more and stopped wearing the hats all together. Sparrows still perch on the top branches of elm trees to tell stories and weave wonderful inventions. They just don't fasten them onto donkeys' heads any more. And the donkeys are glad about that.

"Hee Haw!"

# Summary of folding directions:

Fold a square in half at the diagonal.

**Result: Fold # 1** A Triangle.

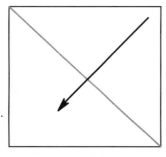

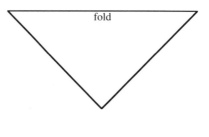

Fold top corners down to lower corner along dashed lines.

**Result: Fold #2** A donkey with long droopy ears.

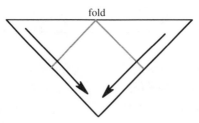

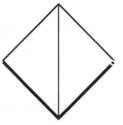

Fold both lower tips up to the top point and crease along the dotted line.

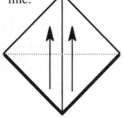

**Result: Fold #3** The ears folded up.

Lift up only the top layer of the bottom point and crease it up at the dotted line.

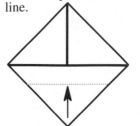

**Result: Fold #4** Ears held with a handband.

Fold only the top layer up, creasing at the dotted line to form a thick band to hold the upper tips in place.

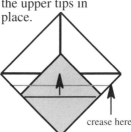

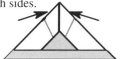

crease here

**Result: Fold #5** A headband that holds the donkey's ears in place.

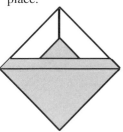

Tuck the back flap up into the center of the hat.

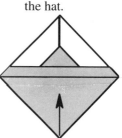

**Result: Fold #6** A hat with no back flap.

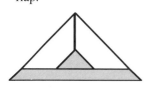

Fold only the top layer back and crease at the dotted line on both sides.

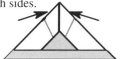

**Result: Fold #7** The completed hat with donkey's ears sticking out.

# Optional applications for "How The Donkey Got His Haw"

1. After telling the story, review the donkey's problems as they relate to the progressive construction of the hat *(auditory memory)*. First the donkey couldn't see because his ears were too long, then he could see, but the headband wouldn't hold his ears, then the hat held his ears, but he couldn't hear. Finally, he could both hear and see and the hat is finished. Construct the hat again *(visual memory)* and let the group tell you which folds come next. Distribute squares of paper and make each fold together as a group *(synthesis)*.

2. Decorate the finished hats, then unfold to see where the decorative marks are on the flat paper. Then decorate flat, unfolded paper and before folding the hats, ask for predictions of where the decorative marks will be on the completed hat *(analysis)*.

3. Plan a hat making party for stuffed animals or dolls. When all the hats are completed, have a parade or dance to show them off.

4. Start with squares of various sizes and ask for predictions of the bottom lengths of the resulting hats. Make a table of the results. Determine the ratios. Extend the calculations up and down and then test the theory by making hats from the various sized squares. Evaluate which sizes are the most practical when comparing the ease of folding to the ease of usage *(analysis, synthesis, evaluation)*.

5. Use this story to introduce or complement discussions or units about:
   a. Hats.
   b. Donkeys.
   c. Birds.
   d. The physical changes animals have experienced throughout history (prehistoric vs. modern).
   e. Frustrations resulting from physical handicaps.
   f. The inventive spirit. What motivates inventions? Trial and error testing?
   g. Animals roaming freely vs. being taken care of (and serving) humans.
   h. Friendship. Helping one another.

6. Research the various versions of this model, referred to as the traditional helmet or a Samurai helmet. It is constructed in a variety of ways and is one of the most common beginning origami folds. A traditional sea bream can be constructed from it with the following steps:

   Begin with the finished hat. Pull the back flap out of the inside of the hat and instead, fold it up to form the back outside of the hat. Then push the outside corners together to fold the hat in half.

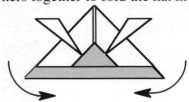

Make 3 cuts: Make a slit along the top fold and both the bottom folds about 2/3 of the way toward the right point. Then fold the resulting flaps along the dotted line to form the fish's tail.

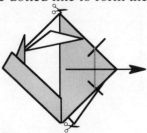

Cut along dotted line on the tail to shape it. Fold the lower point under and into the center on both sides. Push the top in to make a tuck on top for a dorsal fin.

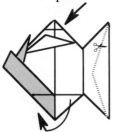

**Result:** The complete traditional sea bream.

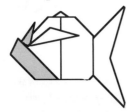

7. Make up funny stories and songs that the brown sparrows might have told. Present them and encourage the group to "Hee-Haw" at the punch lines *(synthesis)*.

| Date | Group | Notes |
|---|---|---|
|  |  |  |
|  |  |  |
|  |  |  |
|  |  |  |
|  |  |  |

This elegant swan is made in six steps. Folding directions begin on page 32.

**About the story:**

A famous kite master goes to great lengths to finally satisfy his most difficult customer.

**Recommended ages:**

Listening and folding:  age 5 through adult.

**Required materials:**

1 square of paper at least 6 inches each side, folded into a swan and then completely unfolded for storytelling.

**Optional introductory statement:**

*I'm going to tell you a story about a very famous kite master and a very grouchy kite flier from the very windy city of Chicago, Illinois. As I tell you the story, watch carefully as I fold paper into various shapes. This is called origami, or Japanese paper folding. Do you have any questions? (pause) The name of the story is "Satisfaction Guaranteed".*

# Satisfaction Guaranteed

A famous kite master owns a little shop along the shore of Lake Michigan in the very windy city of Chicago, Illinois. He is famous because he makes the most colorful, most unusual and most aerodynamic kites in the whole city and possibly in the entire world. This kite master always guarantees his customers that they will be completely satisfied or he will personally fix their kites until they are happy. In all his many years of inventing kites, he's never encountered a dissatisfied customer.

One day not long ago, a grumpy man wearing a plain triangular hat like this *(hold up fold #1)* parked his car along the beach front at Lake Michigan to watch a group of kite fliers.

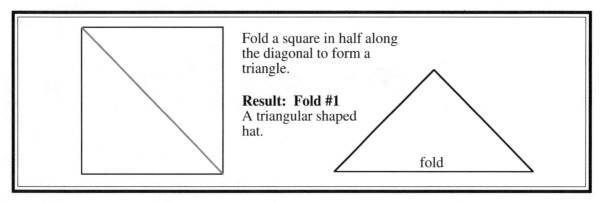

Fold a square in half along the diagonal to form a triangle.

**Result:  Fold #1**
A triangular shaped hat.

fold

The wind was especially gusty that day. Glittering kites of all different shapes and sizes flapped and bobbed with frenzied excitement. Some whirled with flashy propellers and others flitted about with layers of wings and tails.

The kite fliers giggled, their spirits as high as the kites that danced above them. The more they laughed, the more surly and discouraged the grumpy man became. All he could think about was how disappointing his life was. Things never worked out well for him. He was always in trouble at work. No one would go to the movies with him, let alone marry him. And just yesterday, his dog bit him in the leg and ran away from home.

"These kite fliers shouldn't be out here having so much fun while I feel so bad," he mumbled.

Then he read a flashing sign across the beach. SATISFACTION GUARANTEED!!! It was the popular slogan of the famous kite master.

"I've never been satisfied about anything," said the grumpy man. "I think I'll prove that kite master wrong."

He straightened out his triangular hat, drove to the kite shop and marched right up to the counter, determined to show the kite master that it's impossible to satisfy everyone. With a deep frown and snapping eyes, he picked through the selection of colorful flying creations. But they were all too bright and cheery for his tastes.

"Don't you have a plain kite that's just like my triangular hat?" he asked.

"No," said the kite master. "I don't have many requests for plain kites but I could turn your triangular hat into a kite if that would make you happy."

"It won't make *me* happy, but go ahead and try."

So the kite master opened the triangular hat into a flat diamond and folded the outside corners in like this *(demonstrate with fold #2)* to make a rather plain, but practical kite.

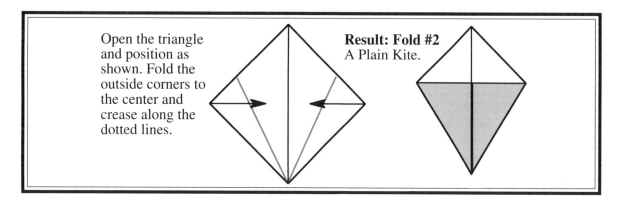

Open the triangle and position as shown. Fold the outside corners to the center and crease along the dotted lines.

**Result: Fold #2**
A Plain Kite.

"Hrumpf.....this is just the kind of kite I had in mind, but I doubt that it will fly," snarled the man. He paid the kite master and took his new kite out to his car.

He saw immediately that his prediction was already true. The kite was too wide to fit into his car. He stomped right back to the famous kite master and shouted, "I am not satisfied! This kite won't even fit through the door of my car!"

"Indeed it won't," agreed the kite master. "I will fix it for you right now so that you will be happy."

The kite master folded the two widest corners into the middle like this *(demonstrate with fold #3 as shown)* to make the kite slimmer so that it easily slid into the grumpy man's car.

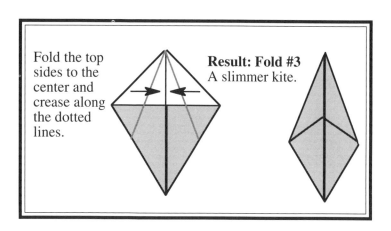

Fold the top sides to the center and crease along the dotted lines.

**Result: Fold #3**
A slimmer kite.

The grumpy man drove back to where the other kite fliers were gathered. He watched them carefully, for he had never flown a kite before and didn't want to make a complete fool out of himself on his first try. It looked easy. The wind did all the work.

"Here goes nothing," said the grumpy man as he tossed his new kite up into the wind. But he was so eager to prove that it wouldn't fly, he forgot to hold onto the string. The kite filled with freedom and sailed off all by itself over the water.

Suddenly the wind paused and the kite crashed down into the waves. Luckily, some boys were wading in the shallow water and were glad to help him retrieve his kite. Just as he had expected, the kite was broken. It folded over like this when it smashed into the water *(demonstrate with fold #4 as shown):*

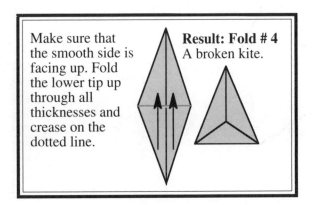

Make sure that the smooth side is facing up. Fold the lower tip up through all thicknesses and crease on the dotted line.

**Result: Fold # 4**
A broken kite.

The man shoved the broken kite into his car and raced back to the famous kite master's little shop.

"I'm not satisfied!" he roared as he threw down the damaged kite.

The kite master figured out immediately what must have happened, for the waters of Lake Michigan were still dripping from the kite and the string was tangled and matted.

"Would you prefer to have a special kite that you don't even have to hold onto? It's made to float in the water."

"I demand satisfaction," sputtered the grumpy man, "and I don't believe that your idea would work."

"We shall see," said the kite master. He hummed a pleasant tune as he folded the entire broken kite in half like this *(demonstrate with fold #5 as shown):*

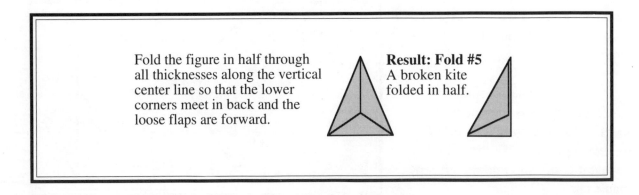

Fold the figure in half through all thicknesses along the vertical center line so that the lower corners meet in back and the loose flaps are forward.

**Result: Fold #5**
A broken kite folded in half.

Then the kite master held the folded kite by its pointed tail and reached inside to pull out another pointed tip. He folded it up like this *(demonstrate with fold #6):*

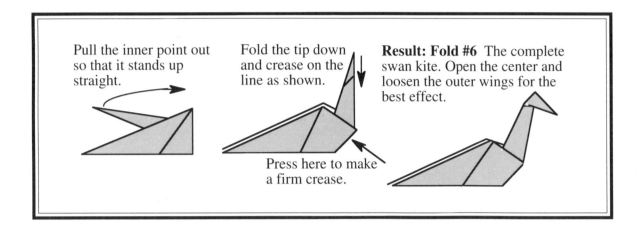

Pull the inner point out so that it stands up straight.

Fold the tip down and crease on the line as shown.

Press here to make a firm crease.

**Result: Fold #6** The complete swan kite. Open the center and loosen the outer wings for the best effect.

"There you go, sir. I believe this kite will make you happy."

"Hrumpf. We shall see," growled the grumpy man as he grabbed the new kite and tossed it into his car for the short drive back to the beach.

When he threw it up into the air, the wind caught the tail of the remodeled kite and lifted it over Lake Michigan. *(Use the swan to dramatize these flying and floating actions).* It dropped gently into the water and bobbed right back to the grumpy man as though eager for another try. The first time this happened, the man's frown loosened up into a little line. After the next flight, he said, "Ah ha!" with a surprised smile. The third time, he actually threw back his head and laughed.

"This is fun!" he shouted and then covered his mouth with shame. He had never laughed out in public before. But nobody paid any attention to him, not even the famous kite master. Everyone assumed that it was just another case of satisfaction guaranteed. And they were right.

# Summary of folding directions:

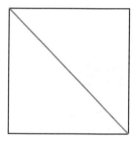

Fold a square in half along the diagonal to form a triangle.

**Result: Fold #1**
A triangular shaped hat.

fold

---

Open the triangle and position as shown. Fold the outside corners to the center and crease along the dotted lines.

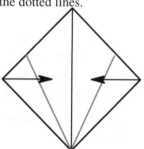

**Result: Fold #2**
A Plain Kite.

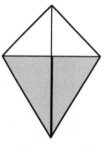

Fold the top sides to the center and crease along the dotted lines.

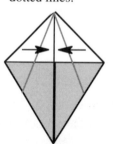

**Result: Fold #3**
A slimmer kite.

---

Make sure that the smooth side is facing up. Fold the lower tip up through all thicknesses and crease on the dotted line.

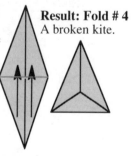

**Result: Fold # 4**
A broken kite.

Fold the figure in half through all thicknesses along the vertical center line so that the lower corners meet in back and the loose flaps are forward.

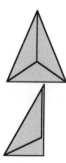

**Result: Fold #5**
A broken kite folded in half.

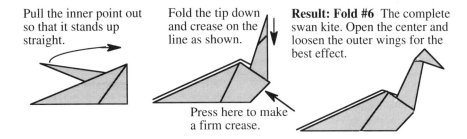

Pull the inner point out so that it stands up straight.

Fold the tip down and crease on the line as shown.

**Result: Fold #6** The complete swan kite. Open the center and loosen the outer wings for the best effect.

Press here to make a firm crease.

# Optional applications for "Satisfaction Guaranteed"

1. Review the different types of kites the grumpy man had and the reasons why each one was unsatisfactory *(auditory memory)*. Reconstruct the swan letting the group tell you which fold comes next *(visual memory)*. Distribute squares of paper and fold each step together as a group *(synthesis)*. Note: Be especially careful that fold #4 is folded with the **smooth** side facing up.

2. Draw feathers and other features on the completed model. Unfold to observe where these markings are on the flat square of paper. Watch the markings come back together as the swan is rebuilt *(analysis)*.

3. Experiment with the aerodynamic qualities of the different folds. Will any of them become airborne? Research the principles involved in flight. Invent a new kite based on those theories *(analysis, synthesis, evaluation)*.

4. Find out why Chicago is known as the "Windy City". Research nicknames for other places and make a puzzle. Write the names of the city on one side and in another order, write the nicknames on the other side. Match the city with its proper nickname individually or as a group *(analysis, evaluation, synthesis)*.

5. Use this story to introduce or complement discussions or units about:
   a. Kite making.
   b. Principles of flight.
   c. Chicago.
   d. Negative and positive expectations.
   e. Swans.
   f. Consumer response to guarantees. Guarantees as a sales technique.
   g. Reputations. How are they formed? How are they changed?
   h. Inventiveness. Persistence.

6. If you have access to water, arrange a swan regatta. Swans made with regular 20# typing paper will float for quite a long time. String the swans together in a long chain or line them up separately. Lightweight objects can ride in them. Divide teams in half, each on opposing sides of the water. Place a button or paper clip (or similar small object) inside the swans and race them across the water. The team member catching the swan removes the object and sends it back to be filled by the next person. When all objects are transported across the water, the relay is done. Several teams can compete or one group can cooperate.

7. Research the various types of origami swans. Compare complexity of construction and the resulting details *(analysis)*. Make the various models and present along with the folding directions *(synthesis)*.

8. An elephant head can easily be made from this model. Start with fold # 5, the broken kite folded in half:

Pull center tip out slightly to form elephant's trunk. Draw eyes on both sides.

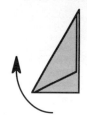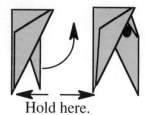

Hold here.

| Date | Group | Notes |
|---|---|---|
|  |  |  |
|  |  |  |
|  |  |  |
|  |  |  |
|  |  |  |

This traditional organ is made in seven steps. Folding directions begin on page 40.

## About the story:

A mouse named Fortissimo (Italian for "very loud") celebrates too loudly when he eats tasty foods, so he decides to find a new home where he is free to celebrate as loudly as he wishes.

## Recommended ages:

Listening only:  age 3 through adult.
Listening and folding:  age 5 through adult.

## Required materials:

1 square of paper at least 6 inches each side, folded into an organ and then completely unfolded for storytelling.

## Optional introductory statement:

*I'm going to tell you a story about a naughty little mouse named Fortissimo. As I tell you the story, watch carefully as I fold paper into various shapes. This is called origami, or Japanese paper folding. Do you have any questions? (pause) The name of the story is "Fortissimo's New Home".*

# Fortissimo's New Home

Mice are simple, peace loving creatures. They live happily in large numbers with very few rules. In fact, there is only one law that all mice must obey. Quiet. Mice must be quiet. Fortunately mice are born with quietness built right in....all mice, that is, except one big-eared gray mouse named Fortissimo.

On the night of his birth, Fortissimo opened his mouth to fill his lungs for the very first time and caused a red alert noise emergency throughout the entire mouse colony. When he exhaled that first breath of air, a single note, loud and shrill, came zinging out of him like a fire alarm in a paper factory....clamorous, shocking and totally unexpected.

Fortissimo tried to be quiet. But his voice was unnaturally loud and his enthusiasm for food was unnaturally great. He could usually squeak out a tiny little "mmmmm," after eating grains of wheat or rice, but a blueberry tasted so yummy to Fortissimo that he just couldn't remember to be quiet. "YUM!" he would shout.

The other mice soon learned that they must never share cookie crumbs with Fortissimo. The sweet crumbs would make him so excited that he actually jumped up and down and sang, "Yahoo! Yahoo!" Finally, the poor noisy mouse was moved down into the deepest darkest room *(hold a flat, unfolded square of paper in the palm of your hand, parallel to the floor to represent the surface of the earth and indicate a place far beneath it to be Fortissimo's new room)* of the colony where even the sharpest cat ears would not hear him.

As Fortissimo grew larger and noisier, more and more food was required to keep him satisfied. The other quiet mice were afraid that Fortissimo would attract unwanted attention from owls and cats if he noisily gathered his own food, so a special guard was posted to make sure that he never left his room far down beneath the surface. He was even noisy while asleep, so his snores were muffled by a tent like this *(hold fold #1 up to resemble a tent)* :

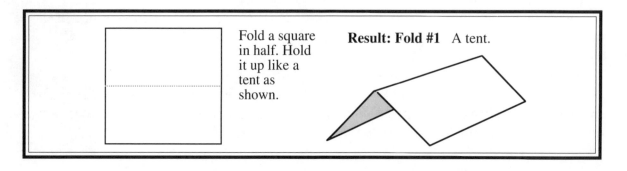

Fold a square in half. Hold it up like a tent as shown.

**Result: Fold #1**  A tent.

Two feeders were always assigned to him, and finally a third was required to scurry away to the storage chambers to bring him more food. Soon all of the activities of the colony revolved around Fortissimo's feeding schedule. When the winter supplies had become dangerously low, the law-abiding, quiet mice began to complain.

"Fortissimo is loud and noisy, but he lives like a king."

"Fortissimo will never learn to be quiet."

"Fortissimo is getting so big we will have to make him a new room."

But before the new construction work was undertaken, Fortissimo decided that it would be better for all of them if he went away to start his own colony in another field. He longed to be free to run in the fields and sing songs to the sun. He didn't want to be a burden and danger to the mice that were working so hard to take care of him.

To help him get a good start, the mice packed up his tent by folding it neatly in half like this *(demonstrate with fold # 2),* and then opening it back up to fold the sides to the center crease.

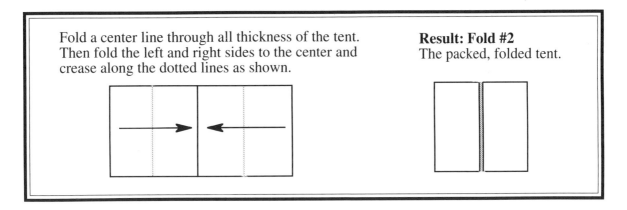

Fold a center line through all thickness of the tent. Then fold the left and right sides to the center and crease along the dotted lines as shown.

**Result: Fold #2**
The packed, folded tent.

His guards and feeders helped him through the long winding tunnel up to the surface.

"Watch out for lights in the night," they warned. "The eyes of cats and owls shine like the moon."

Other mice helped by making a trail of tasty tidbits leading to the other side of the field where they heaped a huge pile of his favorite foods.

When Fortissimo popped his nose out and smelled the sweet crumb trail ahead of him, he forgot all about the dangers he would face. It took his eyes a few minutes to adjust to the bright sunshine, but then he munched contentedly along the crumb trail until he reached the edge of the field.

"The surface is a piece of cake! Not so bad! Not so bad!" he sang when he saw all the good-ies piled up for him at the end of the trail. And how wonderful it was to hear his own voice!

"Hooray!" he shouted. "Yahooooooooooooo!!"

By this time, all the quiet mice of his former colony were long gone and Fortissimo was entirely alone. As he tore into the pile of delicacies, the fresh air and warm sunshine made his eyelids heavy. He fell asleep right there in front of the food, with a blueberry under his tongue.

Much later, he woke up feeling strangely cold and damp. He looked around and was shocked to see two round cat's eyes glaring at him through the darkness. Without a thought, Fortissimo opened his mouth and let out the loudest, most terrified shriek the cat had ever heard.

The cat blinked and stepped back. A real mouse would run away, he thought. A real mouse would never scream or sleep out in the open, snoring so loudly. It must be a trap, thought the cat. I will let some other silly feline be fooled. The cat grinned and slipped away, leaving Fortissimo alone again.

"The surface is a piece of cake! Not so bad! Not so bad!" Fortissimo sang. But then cold wet things began to fall on him. No one had warned him about rain. It felt refreshing at first, but then the drops came down harder and faster. Cold, slimy mud splattered all over his face.

"This is bad! This is bad!" he moaned as he lifted his nose away from the ground to wash off some of the mud. Far off in the distance, he saw a little country church that looked like this (hold *up fold #3 and #4):*

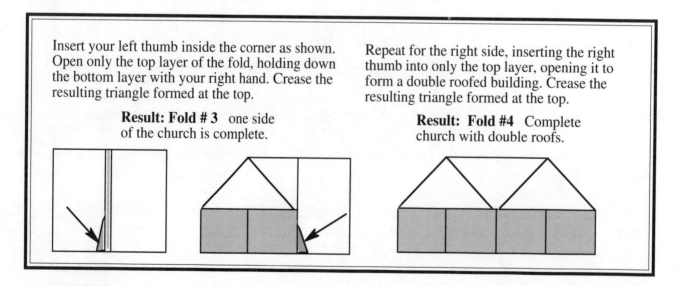

Insert your left thumb inside the corner as shown. Open only the top layer of the fold, holding down the bottom layer with your right hand. Crease the resulting triangle formed at the top.

**Result: Fold # 3** one side of the church is complete.

Repeat for the right side, inserting the right thumb into only the top layer, opening it to form a double roofed building. Crease the resulting triangle formed at the top.

**Result: Fold #4** Complete church with double roofs.

Actually, this country church was not far off at all, but when you are as unused to moving, and as soaked and miserable as poor Fortissimo was, plodding through a downpour to reach shelter seemed like a very great challenge indeed!

As Fortissimo struggled to drag his mud-soaked belly closer to the church, moaning and groaning all the way, he saw that the church had three big steps to climb *(fold the steps of the church as shown, resulting in fold # 5)*:

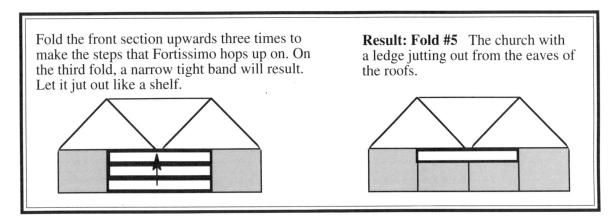

Fold the front section upwards three times to make the steps that Fortissimo hops up on. On the third fold, a narrow tight band will result. Let it jut out like a shelf.

**Result: Fold #5** The church with a ledge jutting out from the eaves of the roofs.

With a mighty effort, Fortissimo lifted his body up one step, and then up a second step, and finally up a third, until he reached the top and flipped himself over the edge, tumbling down inside the church *(slip a finger into the fold and indicate a place inside where Fortissimo landed)*. Fortissimo found a cozy corner that was dry and warm. He covered himself like this *(fold # 6 as shown)*:

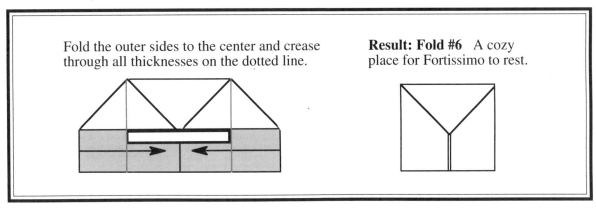

Fold the outer sides to the center and crease through all thicknesses on the dotted line.

**Result: Fold #6** A cozy place for Fortissimo to rest.

Soon he was snoring as loudly as ever. The next morning Fortissimo awoke to the most wonderful sound:

Bing Bong morning song.
Ring - a - ling. Come and sing.
Bing Bong sing along.
Bing Bong sing along.

Then he heard strange tapping and rustling noises all around him. He crept further inside his cozy hide-out. Suddenly the sides swung open like this *(fold #7 as shown)*:

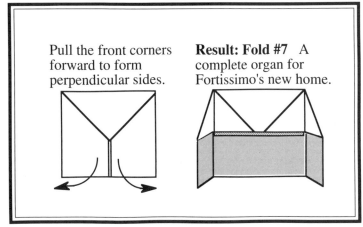

Pull the front corners forward to form perpendicular sides.

**Result: Fold #7** A complete organ for Fortissimo's new home.

Full rich chords filled the air. The music was so loud, even Fortissimo had to cover his ears. But the songs were wonderful and he quickly grew to love his new life in his new home, the church organ. He found plenty to eat, the temperature was always right, it never rained, and best of all, Fortissimo sang his heart out every time the organist came to play.

It isn't known if Fortissimo was the world's first church mouse, but he was certainly the happiest. If you are ever lucky enough to visit a little country church, listen carefully for loud high-pitched squeaks that can be heard every time the organ plays. If these squeaks began mysteriously after a cold rainy night many years ago, then you are probably visiting Fortissimo's new home. And by the way, he'd be thrilled if you left a few extra crumbs at the door on your way out.

# Summary of folding directions:

 Fold a square in half. Hold it up like a tent as shown.

**Result: Fold #1**  A tent.

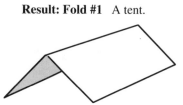

---

Fold a center line through all thickness of the tent. Then fold the left and right sides to the center and crease along the dotted lines as shown.

**Result: Fold #2**
The packed, folded tent.

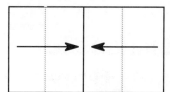

---

Insert your left thumb inside the corner as shown. Open only the top layer of the fold, holding down the bottom layer with your right hand. Crease the resulting triangle formed at the top.

Repeat for the right side, inserting the right thumb into only the top layer, opening it to form a double roofed building. Crease the resulting triangle formed at the top.

**Result: Fold # 3**  one side of the church is complete.

**Result:  Fold #4**  Complete church with double roofs.

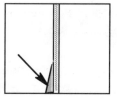 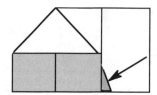

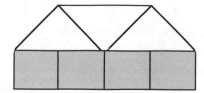

Fold the front section upwards three times to make the steps that Fortissimo hops up on. On the third fold, a narrow tight band will result. Let it jut out like a shelf.

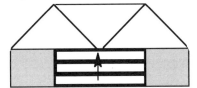

**Result: Fold #5** The church with a ledge jutting out from the eaves of the roofs.

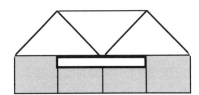

Fold the outer sides to the center and crease through all thicknesses on the dotted line.

**Result: Fold #6** A cozy place for Fortissimo to rest.

Pull the front corners forward to form perpendicular sides.

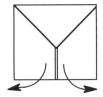

**Result: Fold #7** A complete organ for Fortissimo's new home.

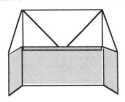

# Optional applications for "Fortissimo's New Home"

1.  After telling the story, review Fortissimo's characteristics that relate to the folds, i.e. Fortissimo's loud snoring led to the tent, his need for leaving led to his tent being folded, his need for shelter led to the church, his need to climb up led to forming the steps, his need for rest led to the cozy bed, and his love of loud singing led to settling on a home in an organ *(analysis)*. Ask the group to identify the cause and effect relationship between Fortissimo's needs and the resulting folds in the order they appeared in the story, reinforcing the visual and auditory associations formed between the story events and the sequence of folds required to construct an organ. Rebuild the organ, letting the group tell you which fold comes next. Distribute squares of paper and construct the organ together as a group *(synthesis)*.

2.  Several parts of the story suggest sounds. Retell the story using body sounds or rhythm

instruments to represent sounds and characters. For example, a shaken tambourine might represent Fortissimo's shrill singing; a rapidly struck triangle, the noise alarm; a woodblock, the first raindrops; a maraca, the pouring rain; or a scraper, Fortissimo's loud snoring. All instruments could play together at the end to represent the many tones of the organ. Record your musical rendition and play it back for the group. During the playback, practice folding the organ. This activity reinforces both auditory and kinesthetic memory and should enable the group to become very proficient at constructing the organ model.

3. Decorate the black and white keys of the finished model and then completely unfold it to see where the decorative marks are on the original square of paper. Fold it into the final form again and watch the decorations reappear in their intended places *(analysis)*. Before unfolding, ask where they think the decorative marks will be on the flat paper *(evaluation)*.

4. Find written music with the word "Fortissimo" on the score. Discuss its Italian meaning, "very loud". Find and define other musical words.

5. Make up a melody for the bell's morning song in small groups or individually. Compare and contrast the different versions. Discuss the reasons some are more effective than others. String them together into one long song or let the group choose one or two to sing as rounds, accompany with rhythm instruments, or develop harmonies for. Create second or third verses *(analysis, synthesis, evaluation)*.

6. Use the story to introduce or complement discussions or units about:
   a. Mice (rodents).
   b. Rules necessary for survival. Regulations that may not be necessary.
   c. Discipline vs. punishment. What works, what doesn't.
   d. Pioneers. Why do people decide to move or settle elsewhere?
   e. The colonization of Australia. The history of famous exiles or outcasts.
   f. Noise tolerance. How does it develop? Why are some more sensitive? Less sensitive?
   g. Survival of the fittest.
   h. Health habits that lead to proper nutrition and exercise.
   i. Alternatives to leaving. What other actions might have worked in the story?
   j. The phrase "church mouse". Where did it originate? Does it apply in a modern world?

| Date | Group | Notes |
|------|-------|-------|
|      |       |       |
|      |       |       |
|      |       |       |
|      |       |       |
|      |       |       |

Rub the points up and down and the little triangle rises to the top. Folding directions begin on page 48.

## About the story:

Andrew and Jessica have trouble sharing their favorite triangular block, so they figure out how to make more triangles. Slight-of-hand and paper magic make the ending a surprise.

## Recommended ages:

Listening only:  age 5 through adult.
Folding and listening:  age 7 through adult.

## Required materials:

1 pair of scissors, and 1 square of paper at least 6 to 10 inches each side, folded through step #4 and then completely unfolded for storytelling. <u>Note</u>: for best results, this paper trick needs to be practiced. Slight-of-hand is important to maintain surprise.

## Optional introductory statement:

*I'm going to tell you a story about a brother and sister who have trouble sharing their blocks. As I tell you the story, watch carefully as I fold paper into various shapes. This is called origami, or Japanese paper folding. Do you have any questions? (pause) The name of the story is "Life At The Top".*

# Life At The Top

*Note: Fold the preliminary folds for the group before you start the story so that the creases are already made. Unfold the square and hold it up to represent a wooden block.*

**Preliminary Folds:** Fold a square in half, then in half again to make four quarters. Then fold the quarters in half again diagonally. Unfold to a flat square.

The life of a wooden block may not be interesting to most people. After all, its actual growing years ended long ago when its host tree was felled by the snarling teeth of a lumberjack's saw. A block no longer tingles after a cool summer's rain, nor sleeps naked through winter's frozen nights. But memories of its growing years still haunt its angled edges, surging across its wavy lines *(point to the crease lines on the square)* like phantom pains shooting through nerves long severed. Sprawling strength and noble beauty were carved deeply into its grains, never to be erased, never to be forgotten.

It's these memories of life at the top of the forest that give wooden blocks their ageless appeal. A wooden block is more than a toy. It enjoys generations of usefulness as it is built and rebuilt into countless creations, as it crashes and tumbles, forms patterns, is chewed and sucked, balances tables and chairs, is lost and found, stacked and thrown, forever facing new challenges.

This triangular-shaped block *(hold up fold #1)* enjoys such a life. It is the most privileged block in the big blue bag that is usually heaped in the back of Andrew and Jessica's toy closet. Andrew is eight and builds great cities and fancy space stations with the blocks. Jessica is four. She likes to stack and crash the blocks, the louder the better, or if she's feeling especially

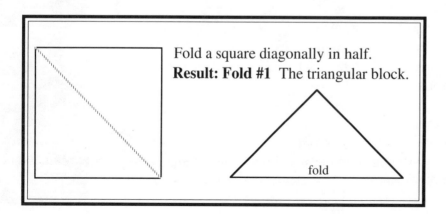

Fold a square diagonally in half.
**Result: Fold #1** The triangular block.

fold

patient, she designs long winding block parades, the different colors and shapes marching all through the room.

This block is special because it is the only triangular shape in their collection. It is used for all the most important things like rooftops, hats, chimneys and rockets. It is always the highest block on top of the stacks.

Andrew doesn't play with the blocks as much as he used to. He is on sport teams now and rides his bike around the neighborhood. He knows all of his friends' telephone numbers by heart and they know his. So he plays with the blocks only if there is absolutely nothing else to do.

But Jessica doesn't know how to ride a bike and isn't allowed to use the telephone without her Mom. So she takes the blocks out every day and has learned how to build windows in her doll houses and roads in her zoos and tall solid walls around her secret hideouts. She especially loves the triangular shaped block and uses it like a crown on top of everything she builds.

One day Andrew refuses to clean his room, so he is not allowed to ride his bike or use the telephone or invite friends over to play. He has nothing else to do, so he decides to play with the blocks. But Jessica is using them. He is shocked at what a good builder she has become. When Jessica leaves her block castle to find some little people to live in it, Andrew can't stop himself.

"Take that!" he says, as he kicks her castle and knocks all the blocks down into one big pile.

When Jessica comes back, he pretends to be sorry. "Oh Jessica, you've got to build the walls stronger so this doesn't happen again. Come on. I'll show you how to build a better castle!"

The two of them work together without arguing or grabbing or pinching until they come to the last piece, the triangular shaped block.

"I want to put it on!" says Jessica.

"No! I'm the oldest! I should put it on!" says Andrew.

"Well I'm the youngest...."

"Well I'm the biggest..."

"I'm the smallest..."

"I'm the smartest..."

Their argument goes on and on until they can't think of any more reasons why they should be the one to place their favorite block.

"I have an idea!" says Andrew. "I'll get my hand saw from the garage and cut it in half. Then we'll both have one."

Andrew gets his handsaw and very carefully cuts the block in half so that he now has two smaller blocks shaped like this *(hold up fold #2)*:

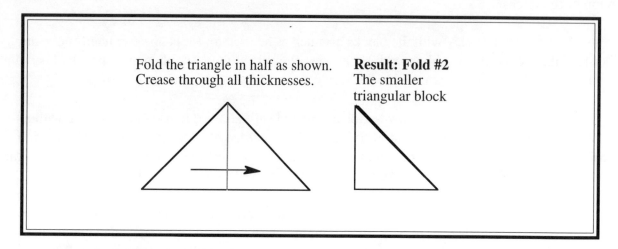

Fold the triangle in half as shown. Crease through all thicknesses.

**Result: Fold #2**
The smaller triangular block

Jessica and Andrew continue to play happily until Andrew notices that the castle could use a pointed block to guard the drawbridge. He takes the new smaller triangular shaped block and imagines an extra corner to it like this *(use your finger to extend the top point of the triangle across and down to the lower corner forming a shape as shown to the right:)*

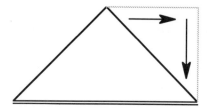

Andrew takes a new rectangular block that he has not cut before and cuts off its corner to get the shape he has imagined to guard the castle drawbridge *(hold up fold #3)*:

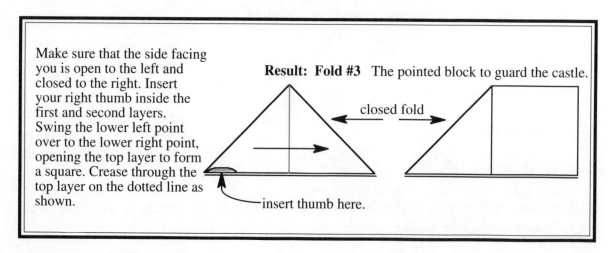

Make sure that the side facing you is open to the left and closed to the right. Insert your right thumb inside the first and second layers. Swing the lower left point over to the lower right point, opening the top layer to form a square. Crease through the top layer on the dotted line as shown.

insert thumb here.

**Result: Fold #3** The pointed block to guard the castle.

closed fold

But he is having so much fun using his saw to create new shapes that he decides that a pointed block is not really practical after all. He gets rid of the point and ends up with a small square like this *(fold #4):*

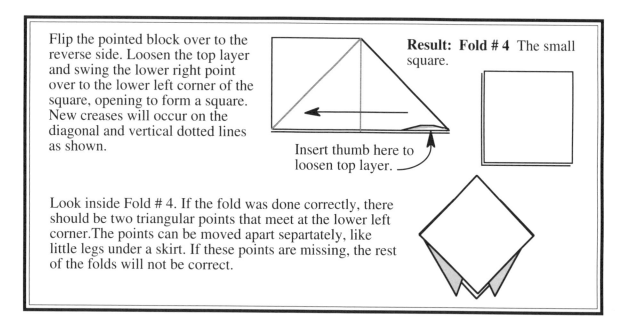

Flip the pointed block over to the reverse side. Loosen the top layer and swing the lower right point over to the lower left corner of the square, opening to form a square. New creases will occur on the diagonal and vertical dotted lines as shown.

Insert thumb here to loosen top layer.

**Result: Fold # 4** The small square.

Look inside Fold # 4. If the fold was done correctly, there should be two triangular points that meet at the lower left corner. The points can be moved apart separtately, like little legs under a skirt. If these points are missing, the rest of the folds will not be correct.

Meanwhile, Jessica can not find her triangular shaped block any where. "Please, Andrew. Won't you cut me a new triangular block?" she begs.

"Sure, I'll make you one right now." He cuts the top corner off the new square like this:

*(Snip off the top corner of the square with a scissors and let the little triangle fall. Without anyone seeing, hide the little triangle in your hand and pretend to look all over for it. When your listeners are distracted by the search, insert the little triangle into the square as shown and begin to rub the points together <u>up and down</u> while you continue the story).*

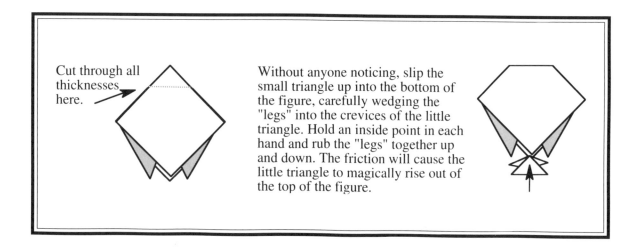

Cut through all thicknesses here.

Without anyone noticing, slip the small triangle up into the bottom of the figure, carefully wedging the "legs" into the crevices of the little triangle. Hold an inside point in each hand and rub the "legs" together up and down. The friction will cause the little triangle to magically rise out of the top of the figure.

"Now where did our new triangular block go?" says Andrew. Jessica and Andrew search and search everywhere. Just as Andrew is about to give up and cut another new triangular block, they look at the top of the pile.

(When you see the tip of the triangle appear, continue with the story).

"Oh look! There it is. On the very top, just where it belongs!"

**The triangle reappears.**

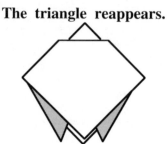

# Summary of folding directions:

**Preliminary Folds:** Fold a square in half, then in half again to make four quarters. Then fold the quarters in half again diagonally. Unfold to a flat square.

Fold a square diagonally in half.

**Result: Fold #1**
The triangular block

fold

Fold the triangle in half. Crease through all thicknesses.

**Result: Fold #2**
The smaller triangular block

Make sure that the side facing you is open to the left and closed to the right. Insert your right thumb inside the first and second layers. Swing the lower left point over to the lower right point, opening the top layer to form a square. Crease through the top layer on the dotted line as shown.

**Result: Fold #3** The pointed block to guard the castle.

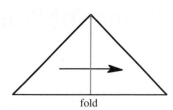

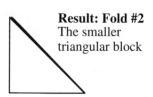

closed fold

insert thumb here.

Flip the pointed block over to the reverse side. Loosen the top layer and swing the lower right point over to the lower left corner of the square, opening to form a square. New creases will occur on the diagonal and vertical dotted lines as shown.

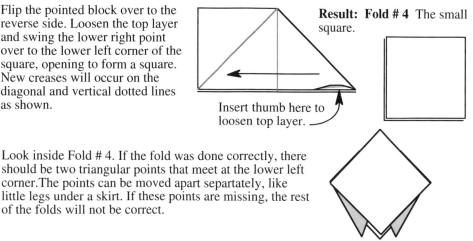

**Result: Fold # 4** The small square.

Insert thumb here to loosen top layer.

Look inside Fold # 4. If the fold was done correctly, there should be two triangular points that meet at the lower left corner.The points can be moved apart separtately, like little legs under a skirt. If these points are missing, the rest of the folds will not be correct.

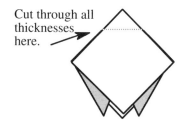

Cut through all thicknesses here.

Without anyone noticing, slip the small triangle up into the bottom of the figure, carefully wedging the "legs" into the crevices of the little triangle. Hold an inside point in each hand and rub the "legs" together up and down. The friction will cause the little triangle to magically rise out of the top of the figure.

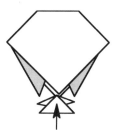

# Optional applications for "Life At The Top"

1. Listeners are always surprised and very eager to learn to make this figure so that they can rush away and amaze people themselves. Review the types of blocks the children played with and the reasons why they made changes *(analysis)*. Andrew cut the triangular block in half so they could stop their argument, he wanted a pointed block to guard the castle, he found it wasn't practical so he cut it into a square, Jessica lost her triangle so he cut her a small one, then it magically reappeared *(auditory memory)*. Rebuild the figure for them *(visual memory)*, letting the group tell you how to proceed. Distribute squares of paper and fold the figure together as a group. *(synthesis)* Note: Beginners often have difficulty with folds #3 and #4. It may be helpful to actually pre-fold the perpendicular midline extending down from the top tip of the triangle (it is notated as a dotted fold line in the directions) before you swing the top layer over to form the square. When the crease is already made, the square easily

falls into place.

2.  A puppet can easily be made from this model:

Fold both outer flaps up as shown.

Fold both of the inside "legs" under as shown.

Add eyes and a chin. Hold with the fingers on top and the thumb on the bottom. The mouth opens and closes to talk.

3.  Use this story to introduce or complement discussions or units on:
    a.  Sharing.
    b.  Cooperation.
    c.  Inventiveness.
    d.  The life cycle of trees.
    e.  Puppetry.
    f.  The historical relationship between magic tricks and paper folding.
    g.  Sibling relationships.
    h.  Jealousy.
    i.  Symbolism, metaphors, similes.

4.  Fold #4 is one of the most basic origami forms. There are many different ways of achieving it. Research the various methods. Compare and contrast the complexity of each method. Determine which is the most effective. Fold other models that can be made starting with this basic form *(analysis, synthesis, evaluation)*.

5.  Give the group a chance to build with actual wooden blocks. Encourage them to create a model or design that they've never tried before *(synthesis)*. After everyone has displayed their creation, have a mini earthquake that knocks everything apart. Rebuild and enjoy the crashing sounds again. The building and rebuilding encourages frustration tolerance and awareness that if something was constructed once, it can always be built again....no big deal.

| Date | Group | Notes |
|------|-------|-------|
|      |       |       |
|      |       |       |
|      |       |       |
|      |       |       |
|      |       |       |

This little dog is made in only two steps. Folding directions begin on page 57.

### About the story:

Animals competed unsuccessfully for years to be the first to climb a mountain. Then a little dog came along with an idea for a new, cooperative approach. But things did not work out exactly as he had planned.....

### Recommended ages:

Listening and folding:  age five through adult.

### Required materials:

1 felt-tipped pen or crayon, 1 square of paper at least 6 inches each side. <u>Note</u>: this is the only model that does not *require* pre-folding. You may pre-fold and then unfold for storytelling if you wish.

### Optional introductory statement:

*I'm going to tell you a story about the problems animals encountered trying to climb a mighty mountain. As I tell you the story, watch carefully as I fold paper into various shapes. This is called origami, or Japanese paper folding. Do you have any questions? (pause) The name of the story is "The Dog And The Mountain".*

# The Dog And The Mountain

Long ago, animals were bolder and more competitive than they are now. All they ever wanted to do, was conquer and control everything on Earth. They climbed every tree, scaled every cliff, swam to every island, crossed every desert, until finally, there was only one mountain left to be defeated. *(Hold up the triangular shape and as you continue with the next sentence and draw a snowy peak on the top point as shown):*

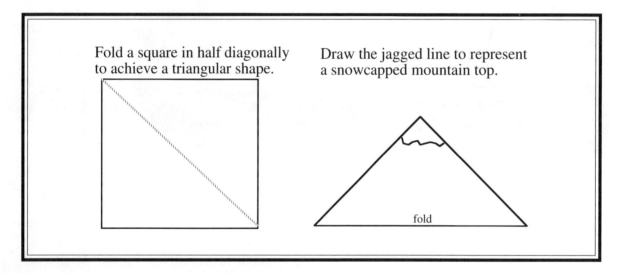

Fold a square in half diagonally to achieve a triangular shape.

Draw the jagged line to represent a snowcapped mountain top.

fold

This, the greatest mountain on Earth, refused to be climbed. Its sheer walls shimmered like mirrors and its crown of crystal ice blazed with glowing radiance. Mighty and terrible, the mountain cast off all who tried to touch its frozen jewels. It reigned supreme for hundreds of years, impossible to climb yet wonderful to behold.

All creatures of the Earth, large and small, winged and footed, clever and brave, stubborn and mischievous...all creatures journeyed to the mountain to test its strength and challenge its dominance. The animals believed that if the mountain could be climbed all the way to its icy top, then the whole world could be seen from this, the mightiest of thrones. From here the animals would gain enough wisdom and power to begin a new age of superiority over nature, an age where they truly would control everything on Earth.

As more and more animals failed in their climb to the top, even more came to watch them fail. Souvenir sellers, mostly of the fox family, and food vendors, mostly squirrels and mice, made tremendous sales and grew in wealth and numbers. The hotels, motels and resorts surrounding the mountain were booked months in advance. They built ponds, caves, deserts, jungles....all for the comfort of the creatures coming to conquer the mountain.

Some attempts were legendary. A noble condor, one of the world's largest birds, was the most famous competitor of all time. He sprang up amidst clamorous cheers, quacks, hoots and screeches so deafening that it was many minutes before the echo finally faded. Then anxious silence settled in until a songbird scout energized the crowd with reports that their hero had rounded the mountain once and was advancing for a second spiral toward the top. As he flew higher, the owls reported that he still looked strong, wisely gliding whenever possible to save his strength. And as the condor's spirals became tighter and shorter, the sharp-eyed eagles reported that he seemed to be laboring for air, but that his wings were still sweeping him to their goal. He was almost there!

Soon the condor was only a black speck against the pure white snow of the mountain top. The great bird stretched his neck up and around, the sharp point of the highest peak within sight. But the cruel chill of the mountain began to freeze his mighty wings, ice and snow weighing down the feathers, his breath hardening to harsh snowdrops that pinged down with ominous warning.

"Go back. Go back," the snowdrops chanted as they struck the cold rock.

Too exhausted to continue, the condor's talons curled and froze shut. The bird fell like a cannon ball released in mid air, plummeting with such force that it gouged out a cave midway down the slope *(draw a circle and color it in as shown)*.

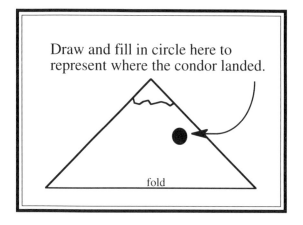

Draw and fill in circle here to represent where the condor landed.

fold

Another historic attempt was made by a contingent of tree frogs gathered from throughout the world. Thousands swarmed the mountain. They formed a kaleidoscope of chirping color, clinging with tiny suction fingers to the sheer vertical cliffs. Smack, smack, smack....the vast army edged upwards, one inch at a time, the eerie rhythm of their struggles uniting them with solid determination.

But the crusaders were foiled by the very nature they sought to defeat. As their tiny fingers touched the cold upper region, their blood thickened and stood still, the frogs tricked into endless hibernation by the mountain's icy shield. The sleeping frogs tumbled down the center of the mountain, blazing a trail that never disappeared *(draw a line to represent the tree frog stain as shown)*.

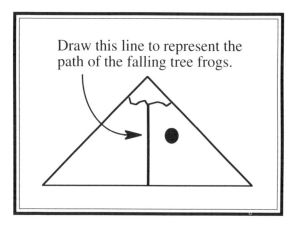

Draw this line to represent the path of the falling tree frogs.

Many years later, a friendly little floppy-eared dog came to the famous mountain, grinning and wagging, his tongue hanging out as he snooped around and mixed freely with all the different animals. He pranced between them, learning all that was known about how not to climb the mountain. Even the suspicious mountain cats and arrogant big horned sheep shared their experiences with the little dog. He was no threat to anyone. Everyone knew that of all the animals on earth, dogs were the very worst climbers.

After the friendly little floppy-eared dog had visited all the animals, he announced, "You have all convinced me that the mountain is impossible to conquer. But what if we could change the shape of the mountain and make it easier to climb? If I can figure out how to change the mountain, would you all agree to let me lead the rest of you up to victory? Would you agree to let me be the king?"

The animals thought that this was the funniest joke ever told. Imagine...the friendly little floppy-eared dog as king! After tremendous belly-aching laughter, one of the land tortoises who had lived there for many years, cleared his throat and croaked, "Give the pup a chance! It sounds like a good idea to me!"

Within hours, a "Change the Mountain!" campaign was launched. The friendly little floppy-eared dog's plan was simple. If every living thing would jump up and down around the mountain at the same time, then perhaps together they could change its shape, tumbling the highest peak, leveling the steepest slopes, cracking the cliffs, chipping steps up to its greatest height.

This plan had wide appeal. It was simple, logical, and it restored hope and cooperation among all of the different animals. When the day of mutual jumping finally arrived, the greatest crowd of all time had assembled around the base of the mountain. Not every creature on earth was there, but the friendly little floppy-eared dog thought that there were enough present to create a great change.

The countdown began and the animals all poised themselves for jumping. 5 - 4 - 3 - 2 - 1......JUMP!

At first there didn't seem to be any effect at all and the animals giggled at how ridiculous they all looked jumping up and down. But before they could complain about what a silly plan it was, a rumble welled up from the very center of the earth. Those with the most sensitive hearing screamed, sparking a wide-eyed stampede away from the mountain.

As the animals turned and fled, the ground began to shake with fearsome power. Huge slabs of rock fell into the crowds as the mountain began to crumble. When the last stone had settled, the bravest animals tiptoed out of their hiding places to find that the friendly little floppy-eared dog had been right!

The mountain was changed! But it had changed for the worse, not the better! Now, instead of just one single peak to conquer, there were three! The tallest center peak was still intact, but now there were two lesser guardians posted at each side like this (*fold the triangle as shown*).

54

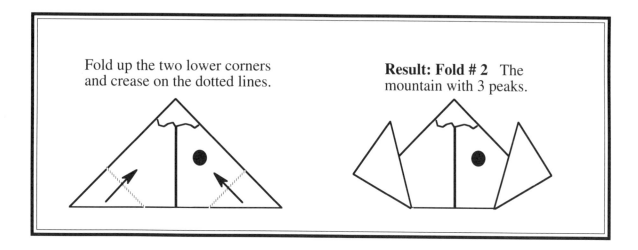

Fold up the two lower corners and crease on the dotted lines.

**Result: Fold # 2** The mountain with 3 peaks.

As you can imagine, the jumpers were greatly disappointed. Now they were worse off than if they had done nothing at all. The snarling mountain cats didn't hang their heads for long. They sent out their best hunters to catch the friendly little floppy-eared dog, but he had already been surrounded by an angry pride of lions. He barked out one last plea.

"Please! Listen to me! We took a risk and faced terrible danger. But look at what we accomplished! We moved the Earth! We made new mountains! If we tried again, I just know we'd have success. After all, if we can make mountains, we can tear them down!"

The lions stopped snarling.

"Never forget!" barked the desperate little dog. "If you're not part of the solution, then you're part of the problem!"

Silence fell over the angry crowd. It was true. Together, they had done an amazing thing. Perhaps they should give him another chance....just *one* more chance.

And so it was agreed that Jump Day II would be scheduled. But this time, *all* of the creatures in the world would be required to participate.

The fox families who sold souvenirs were thrilled about all their new customers. The mice and squirrels worked endlessly gathering food to sell and the resort, hotel and motel businesses had never been better. A week before Jump Day II, the vendors and business owners threw a big party for themselves to celebrate their wonderful successes. In the midst of their congratulations, one somber voice said, "It's too bad all this good fortune is about to end."

"What?" shouted several disbelieving squirrels. "Business has never been better!"

"Yes, but if the friendly little floppy eared dog is right and the mountain is conquered, no one will have a reason to come here any more. We'll all be out of business in less than a year."

They all sat down to consider having to start new lives. Their families had always served customers at the base of the mountain.

Where would they go? What would they do? How would they survive?

"We can't let the mountain be conquered," squeaked a frightened little mouse. "Let's take action."

Jump Day II arrived and all the world's creatures were set and ready to help. Worried merchants and business owners were scattered through the crowds. They had a plan of their own.

A lone raven crowed five times, the signal to begin counting. All the different animals chanted together, howling and growling, peeping and croaking, honking and hissing...all voices united: 5 - 4 - 3 - 2 -1..... JUMP!

All animals joined in, except for the strategically placed merchants and business owners. Instead of helping, they sat down and put their feet up. Then they pointed and laughed at the jumpers around them, making them feel embarrassed. They sat down too, and made fun of other jumpers, who also became embarrassed and sat down. Soon, all the animals were sitting down, pointing and laughing at the brave few who didn't care what anyone else thought of them.

Jump Day II was not a total failure. The first jumps were sufficient to set off new earth tremors, but the jumping did not last long enough to topple the three mountain tops. The tremors did change the mountain, though. After the dust had settled, the animals looked up to see the same center peak, the same side mountains, the usual dark trail made by the tree frogs, and the same old cave made by the

Draw a circle and fill it in here.

crashing condor. What was different was that a new cave had been opened up like this (*draw another circle and fill it in as shown*).

The animals were so puzzled by the joyous celebrations of the merchants, and the mysterious appearance of the new cave that it was several days before they began to ask about what had happened to the friendly little floppy-eared dog. It was generally believed that he ran away in shame, never to return, or that the lions finally did eat him for supper. A few years later, some baby monkeys who liked to swing from their tails and look up at the fierce and mighty mountain discovered what had really happened to the friendly little floppy-eared dog.

After all, hadn't he insisted that if you're not part of the solution, then you become part of the problem?

(*If no one catches on that the mountain is the little dog, invert the figure for them. Most likely, someone in the audience will tell you to turn it upside down.*)

# Summary of folding directions:

Fold a square
diagonally in half.

Fold both lower
corners up as shown.

Invert for the complete dog.

# Optional applications for
# "The Dog And The Mountain"

1. Review the two folding steps required to form the face and ears *(auditory memory)*. Reconstruct the little dog, allowing the group to tell you how to proceed *(visual memory)*. Distribute squares of paper and fold the face and ears together as a group *(synthesis)*. Encourage each participant to add unique or original facial features so that each figure is different than the others.

2. Attach a popsicle stick to hold up like a puppet. Cut out the eyes and attach string to secure like a mask. Open the fold slightly and wear it like a hat. Organize a parade to show off the different designs and decorations.

3. Sponsor a Jump Day. Ask everyone to jump up and down at the same time and observe the results. Compare jumping surfaces and locations. Did windows rattle? Did footprints form in the sand? Did anything fall off of the shelf? Were waves created? *(analysis)*

4. Organize silly relays and contests, letting the dogs compete.

5. Design a publicity campaign the animals might have used to spread the word about Jump Day I or II. Decide which persuasive techniques work most effectively. Apply these same techniques to a realistic cam-

paign that the group feels strongly about *(analysis, application, synthesis, evaluation)*.

6. Use this story to introduce or complement discussions or units about:
   a. Problem solving techniques.
   b. Cooperation.
   c. Sabotage.
   d. Positive and negative expectations.
   e. Animal families. (Characteristics, similarities, differences)
   f. Competition. Winning and losing.
   g. The rights of a few vs. the rights of many.
   h. Advertising principles and techniques.
   i. Folklore. How do legends develop?
   j. Tourist attractions. Hype or substance?

7. Identify the leadership characteristics portrayed by the little dog. Evaluate why he was both successful and unsuccessful. List other possible ways the animals might have conquered the mountain *(analysis, synthesis, evaluation)*.

8. Compare the mountain in the story to a personal, social, or political problem that also seems insurmountable. Find other symbols in the story. Evaluate the use of metaphor as a literary technique.

| Date | Group | Notes |
| --- | --- | --- |
|  |  |  |
|  |  |  |
|  |  |  |
|  |  |  |
|  |  |  |

This rabbit is constructed in seven easy steps. Folding directions begin on page 66.

## About the story:

Jerome loves to pretend! When his big brother doesn't show up to walk him home from school, Jerome has the adventure of his life!

## Recommended ages:

Listening only: age 4 through adult.
Folding and listening: age 7 through adult.

## Required materials:

1 square of paper at least 6 inches each side, folded into a rabbit, and then completely unfolded for storytelling.

## Optional introductory statement:

*I'm going to tell you a story about the after school adventures of an imaginative boy named Jerome. As I tell you the story, watch carefully as I fold paper into various shapes. This is called origami, or Japanese paper folding. Do you have any questions? (pause) The name of the story is "Jerome's After School Adventure".*

# After School Adventure

Grand adventures and daring exploits are all Jerome B. Cartwright ever thinks about. When his teacher tells him to spell, "September," he writes *surrender*. When his mother says, "Be polite!", he thinks she says, *"Be a pirate!"*

Jerome loves to imagine himself as a conquering warrior or an exploring hero, and he's always on the lookout for real-life adventures. But nothing extraordinary ever happens to him, especially when he is with his big brother, Anthony G. Cartwright who is in Junior High School and tall for his age. Big brother Anthony hates to pretend and is always telling Jerome, "Hurry up and stop daydreaming!"

Every day after school, Anthony waits with the other big brothers and sisters outside Jerome's elementary school so that they can all walk home together. They always pass a flat parking lot that looks like this *(hold up the square of paper to represent the parking lot and then begin making the preliminary folds indicated in fold #1 as you continue telling the story).*

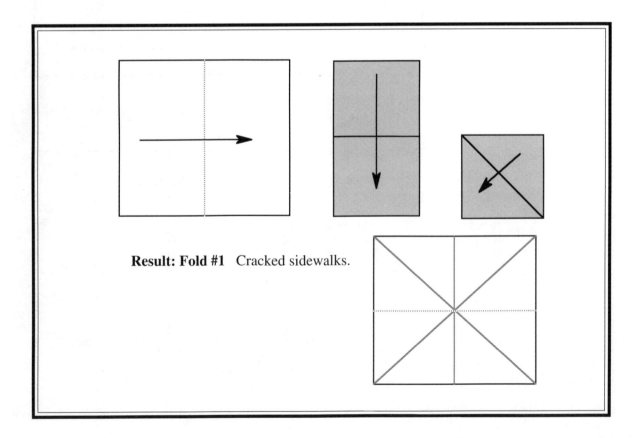

**Result: Fold #1**  Cracked sidewalks.

Then they walk by rows of little shops with windows decorated with toys and candy, flowers and books, and all kinds of ladies' dresses. The fun begins when they come to a section where the sidewalks are cracked with lines crisscrossing all over like this *(hold up fold #1)*.

Sometimes Jerome steps on every line *(jump your fingers from line to line on the paper)* and sometimes Jerome tries not to step on any *(jump your fingers in the spaces)*. Lines or no lines, big brother Anthony always rushes on ahead because he can't wait to get home to eat a peanut butter sandwich before he goes out to play basketball with his friends.

Anthony yells, "Quit hopping around like a rabbit, Jerome! If you don't keep up, I'm going to leave you!"

Jerome hurries then, because even though they take the same route down Fifth Street every day, the farther they go, the more the buildings look alike. They are all high and narrow with tall double doors that open like this *(open and close the tall doors of fold # 2):*

> Fold the outer sides to the center fold and crease along the dotted lines as shown:
>
> **Result: Fold #2**
> Tall Double Doors.

Finally as the two brothers are almost home, they come to a high- backed bench that is right across the street from their apartment building. It looks like this *(hold up fold #3)*:

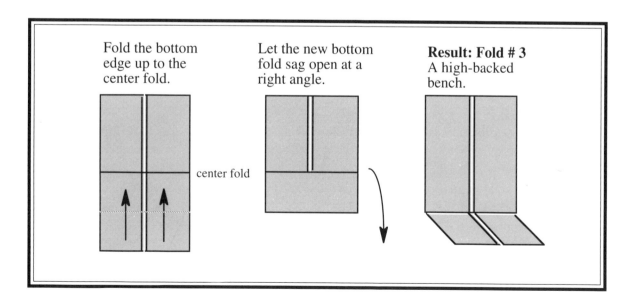

Fold the bottom edge up to the center fold.

center fold

Let the new bottom fold sag open at a right angle.

**Result: Fold # 3**
A high-backed bench.

One rainy day at Junior High School, big brother Anthony tries to throw a note across the room to his friend. Unfortunately, his friend is paying attention to the teacher instead of to Anthony so the note sails all the way to the front of the room and hits the teacher right in the face. Anthony has to stay after school to clean chalkboards and staple a pile of papers. He can not leave until he has finished, not even to go to pick up his little brother, Jerome.

When Jerome gets out of school and is ready to walk home as usual, Anthony is not there to help him. He is still at Junior High School stapling papers. But Jerome doesn't know that. He thinks something adventurous must have happened because Anthony has never missed walking him home before.

"I'd better hurry home to find out what kind of daring exploit  Anthony is having without me!" he says.

Jerome runs past the old parking lot, waves at his reflection in the little shop windows, and then hops over all the lines in the cracked sidewalks. It isn't until he reaches the high-backed bench that he notices anything out of the ordinary. There on the bench sits a kind old woman wearing a wide-brimmed straw hat that looks like this *(hold up fold # 4 and point to the top portion):*

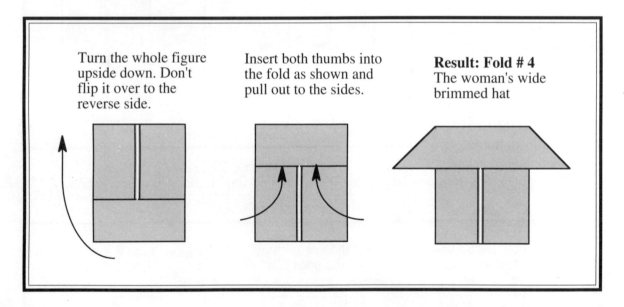

Turn the whole figure upside down. Don't flip it over to the reverse side.

Insert both thumbs into the fold as shown and pull out to the sides.

**Result: Fold # 4**
The woman's wide brimmed hat

She almost seems to be waiting for Jerome, for as he approaches, she looks up and smiles at him very mysteriously.

Just then, a sudden gust of wind sweeps the wide-brimmed hat off her head and sends it tumbling down the sidewalk. *(Demonstrate with the fold tumbling away).* Jerome leaps after it, scoops it up and returns it to the kind old woman at the high backed bench.

"You are my hero," she says with a graceful curtsy. "Your quick actions today tell me that you must be a boy who loves adventure. Am I right, young man?"

"Yes, ma'am," says Jerome, his eyes widening.

"What type of adventure does a hero like you enjoy?"

Jerome shrugs. "I think being a pirate is fun."

She leans closer to him and whispers, "I believe you are about to have the adventure of your life, young man. All your wishes will come true today! Remember this forever! It is always good luck to help an old woman when the wind blows off her hat!"

Then she pulls her wide-brimmed hat down low on her head and points a wrinkled finger up to the roof of Jerome's apartment building. "Mighty fancy roof on your building," she says.

Jerome looks up to see that the roof is decorated like this *(hold up fold # 5)* and the old woman and her hat slip away, never to be seen again.

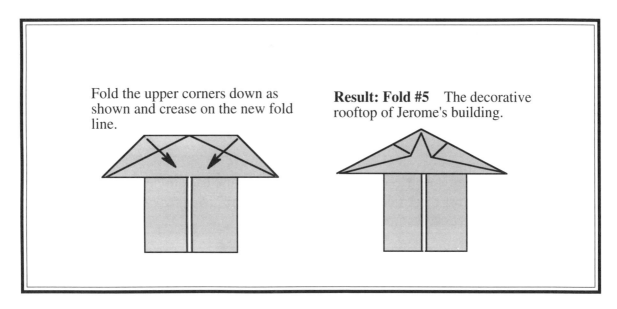

Fold the upper corners down as shown and crease on the new fold line.

**Result: Fold #5**  The decorative rooftop of Jerome's building.

All of a sudden a jagged bolt of lightening zips through the sky. BAM! Rain pours down and Jerome is soaked before he can run to the tall double doors of his building. The rain is pounding down so hard that he can't even pull the door open. Fifth Street fills with water. It is a little brook at first, but as more water gushes up out of the drains, the street swells into a raging river, tumbling over the curbs and up the steps leading to all the tall narrow buildings.

It seems like Jerome's world has turned upside down *(invert fold #5 and let it bob along like a boat)* when, suddenly, a ship with a great wide smoke stack floats up to the steps.

"Jolly Rogers! It's my adventure!" he shouts as he leaps aboard to examine the throttle and engine controls. "I don't know how to drive a steam ship. I wish this was an old fashioned pirate ship with a huge billowing sail."

And before he can say 'Shiver me timbers', the engines disappear and the smoke stack turns into a sail like this *(hold up fold #6):*

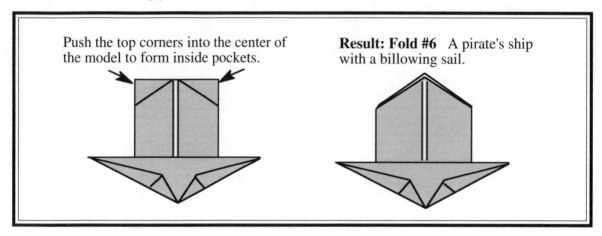

Push the top corners into the center of the model to form inside pockets.

**Result: Fold #6** A pirate's ship with a billowing sail.

Away goes Jerome, floating down Fifth Street toward City Lake Park. But the lake is flooded and water hides all but the tallest trees in the park. These treetops look like islands dotting the edge of a boiling sea.....Jerome's sea, waiting to be explored and conquered.

"Ahoy! I claim this island for my pirate fort!" he declares as he gets out at the closest treetop. But when he steps out to arrange the branches and leaves into a fortress wall, his ship slips off and drifts across the flooded lake *(demonstrate with the model floating away)* until it docks at another group of treetop islands.

"Bad luck," says Jerome. "How will I ever get my treasure back to home port now? I wish I could hop like a rabbit across those treetops to get back my ship!" *(Begin shaping fold #7 and continue as the story progresses until the rabbit is formed).*

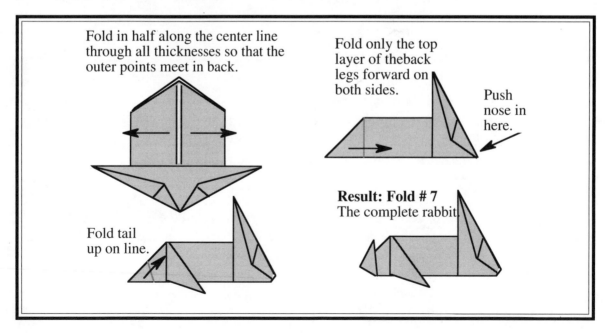

Fold in half along the center line through all thicknesses so that the outer points meet in back.

Fold only the top layer of theback legs forward on both sides.

Push nose in here.

Fold tail up on line.

**Result: Fold # 7** The complete rabbit

Before he can say 'Hippity hop', Jerome gets a sudden powerful craving for a leafy green salad.  He now has long pointed ears like this, *(demonstrate on the rabbit fold and adjust each part as you describe it in the story)* strong hind legs, and a cute little cottonball tail. He doesn't waste any time admiring his new bunny self. Jerome the Giant Rabbit leaps from treetop to treetop over the raging waters until he lands at his ship with a mighty splash.

"I wish I was a pirate captain again," he commands, and before he can say 'pass the salad dressing', he is back in his ship, steering away from the flooded park *(unfold the rabbit back to the sailing ship in fold #6).*

As Jerome sails back down Fifth Street to his home port, he can't wait to compare adventures with his big brother Anthony. He finally spies the fancy roof of their building *(unfold to #5)* and shouts, "Land ahoy!"

When Jerome moors his ship at the steps, there is still too much water for him to open the tall double doors to his building.

"I wish this water would dry up so I can get inside," he says.

Before he can say 'man overboard', the ship vanishes and the street returns to normal.

*(Unfold to fold #2 and open the doors.)*

Jerome pulls open the great double doors leading to his apartment and runs up two flights of stairs just in time to find Anthony fumbling with his key in the lock.

"Hurry up, Jerome! Stop daydreaming! I'm starving!" complains Anthony as he hurries inside to make a peanut butter sandwich.

Jerome fixes himself a big salad. Grand adventures and daring exploits really work up an appetite.

# Summary of folding directions:

**Preliminary Folds:** Fold a square in half, then in half again to make four quarters. Then fold the quarters in half again diagonally. Unfold to a flat square.

---

Fold the outer sides to the center fold and crease along the dotted lines as shown:

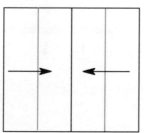

**Result: Fold #2**
Tall Double Doors.

---

Fold the bottom edge up to the center fold.

center fold

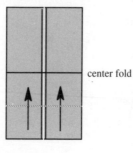

Let the new bottom fold sag open at a right angle.

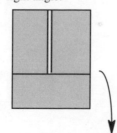

**Result: Fold # 3**
A high-backed bench.

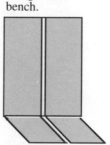

Turn the whole figure upside down. Don't flip it over to the reverse side.

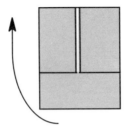

Insert both thumbs into the fold as shown and pull out to the sides.

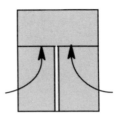

**Result: Fold # 4** The woman's wide brimmed hat

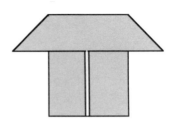

---

Fold the upper corners down as shown and crease on the new fold line.

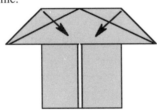

**Result: Fold #5** The decorative rooftop of Jerome's building.

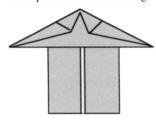

---

Push the top corners into the center of the model to form inside pockets.

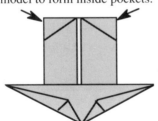

**Result: Fold #6** A pirate's ship with a billowing sail.

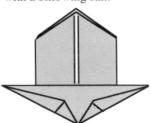

---

Fold in half along the center line through all thicknesses so that the outer points meet in back.

Fold only the top layer of theback legs forward on both sides.

Push nose in here.

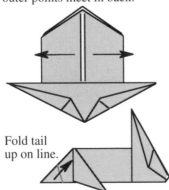

Fold tail up on line.

**Result: Fold # 7** The complete rabbit.

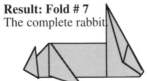

# Optional applications for "After School Adventure"

1. After telling the story, ask your listeners to name in order all of the things the boys normally pass on their way home from school *(auditory memory)*. Then ask them to recall the order of the seven folds required to make the rabbit *(visual memory)*. As you construct the rabbit for them again, let them tell you what the next steps will be, using the descriptive names from the story (i.e., the cracked sidewalk, the tall double doors, the high backed bench, etc.). Distribute squares of paper and construct the rabbit together as a group, again relating each step to the story *(synthesis)*. Ask, "What kind of sidewalks did Jerome jump around on?" "What kind of doors did the buildings have?" "What did the old woman lean against?" etc. The more these associations are reinforced, the more memory is enhanced.

2. It is often interesting to decorate the finished model and then completely unfold it to see where the decorative marks are on the original square of paper. Fold it into the final form again and watch the decorations reappear in their intended places *(analysis)*. Before unfolding, predict where the decorative marks will be on the flat paper *(evaluation)*.

3. Use this story to lead into or complement units on:
   a. Sibling relationships.
   b. The courage required to express imaginative ideas.
   c. Safety rules for walking to and from school.
   d. Different types of homes people live in.
   e. Fantasy vs. reality. What parts of the story could really happen?
   f. Rainy day activities.
   g. Pirates and sailors.
   h. Rabbits.

4. Act out Jerome's adventure as a group *(kinesthetic memory)*. Pantomime the actions and reactions. Let each listener take a part and finish by having a peanut butter sandwich and lettuce salad party.

5. Dance the "Bunny Hop".

6. Divide the listeners and their rabbits into teams for rabbit relays and silly hopping contests.

7. Punch holes into the rabbits and lace with yarn for necklaces, ornaments, or bracelets.

| Date | Group | Notes |
|------|-------|-------|
|      |       |       |
|      |       |       |
|      |       |       |
|      |       |       |
|      |       |       |

This versatile pinwheel (windmill) is made in 6 steps. Folding directions begin on page 74.

**About the story:**

Jerome blasts off in homemade space machines and does battle with imaginary space invaders. Finally he zooms away with his spinning propeller to rescue the city from alien strawberry slush rays!

**Recommended ages:**

Listening only:  age 3 through adult.
Listening and folding:  age 5 through adult.

**Required materials:**

1 pencil or pen with a sharp point to insert into the pinwheel, and 1 square of paper at least 6 inches each side, folded into a pinwheel and then completely unfolded for story telling. For spinning pinwheels, avoid wrapping paper or papers with similar limp textures.

**Optional introductory statement:**

*I'm going to tell a story about the adventures of a boy who wakes up one Saturday morning and discovers that his city has been taken over by alien space invaders! As I tell you the story, watch carefully as I fold paper into various shapes. This is called origami, or Japanese paper folding. Do you have any questions? (pause) Up, up and away! To the rescue!*

# To The Rescue

One Saturday morning in January, Jerome B. Cartwright wakes up to a changed world! Everything outside is covered by a thick blanket of new white snow *(demonstrate with a plain white unfolded square of paper)*.

"Hey, Anthony! Get up! Look out the window! Alien spaceships dropped a cosmic powder bomb all over the city!" Jerome presses his face against the cold glass.

"Hey, Anthony! No one is out plowing away the space dust! The space invaders must have captured all of the city's anti-invader crews!"

He nudges his big brother who is buried under the patchwork quilt their Grandma made them for Christmas. "Hrumpf nah," mumbles Anthony as he rolls over to cover his head.

Not a good sign. Ever since Anthony entered Junior High and became tall for his age, he began sleeping until noon every Saturday. The two brothers used to play together all the time, but now all Anthony wants to do is eat, shoot baskets, and call Jerome names like "pest, twerp, and weirdo". Even alien space invaders are friendlier than Anthony now days. So Jerome activates his silencer and tiptoes to his dresser to change into a fresh space uniform without bothering his big brother any more.

He pours himself some moon juice and a bowl of crater wafers, then pops some Pluto shingles into the toaster. His internal battery pack is recharged in less time than it takes an alien space ship to zoom around the city. And by the height of the space powder drifts outside, Jerome knows that there must be some pretty powerful aliens hovering around!

Jerome pulls on his silver space pants and thick soled moon boots. Silver gloves, a black hat and a gray jacket complete his uniform. He is all set to rescue the city from the chilling effects of the cosmic space powder!

Clumping and rustling down the stairs, he pulls open the great double doors of his space station like this, *(demonstrate with fold #1)* steps out, and...OOPS!

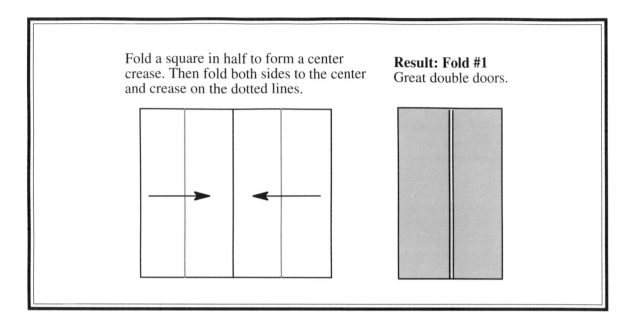

Fold a square in half to form a center crease. Then fold both sides to the center and crease on the dotted lines.

**Result: Fold #1**
Great double doors.

The aliens left a slippery trap for him! Down he goes, rolling and sliding on the wheelchair ramp *(show fold #2 and slide your hand down the steep incline of the fold)* like a comet zipping through an icy chute.

"You won't conquer me!" shouts Jerome as he charges back up the steps to the top of the icy ramp.

BLAST OFF! He's down again. And again! And again! When Jerome has finally been launched into space enough times, he decides that what he really needs is a mini space shuttle so that he can cruise around the city to locate the alien headquarters. He finds a piece of cardboard and folds both sides up like this *(demonstrate with fold #3)* :

Jerome jumps into the commander's chair and prepares to take off. But something is wrong.

"Commander to engine room. Give me a status report. Why aren't we moving? Too

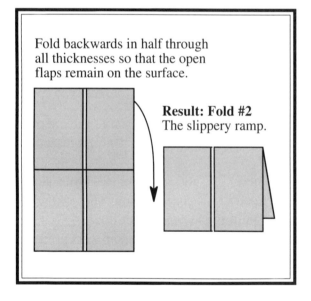

Fold backwards in half through all thicknesses so that the open flaps remain on the surface.

**Result: Fold #2**
The slippery ramp.

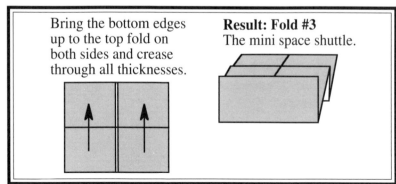

Bring the bottom edges up to the top fold on both sides and crease through all thicknesses.

**Result: Fold #3**
The mini space shuttle.

much gravity, you say? Launching not possible in this vehicle? Don't wait another nanosecond! Prepare the anti-gravitational space sled!" he shouts.

Jerome climbs out of the cardboard space shuttle to make repairs before the evil space invaders can capture him and turn his blood into frosty strawberry slush. He sticks his index fingers into the space shuttle like this and pulls out all the corners like this *(demonstrate with fold #4):*

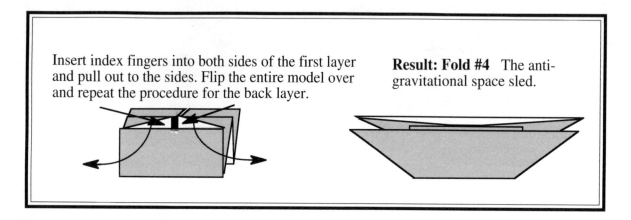

Insert index fingers into both sides of the first layer and pull out to the sides. Flip the entire model over and repeat the procedure for the back layer.

**Result: Fold #4** The anti-gravitational space sled.

Now Jerome can glide through the cosmic space dust at super speeds and rescue the city. He pulls the anti-gravitational space sled up to the top of Fifth St. Hill, climbs in, fastens his safety belts, checks the controls and turns on the intercom.

"This is Commander Jerome. We are off on a dangerous mission to capture the space aliens and secure the city. Prepare for the countdown. 10-9-8-7-6-5-4-3-2-1-BLAST OFF!"

Whew! The anti-gravitational space sled soars down the space walk all the way back to the launching pad of his space station. The cold wind burns his cheeks and stings his eyes. He adjusts his helmet by pulling the rim further down on his forehead and jumps out of the space craft. Oh no! Enemy space buses and alien land rovers are approaching, skidding and spinning toward Fifth Street. Jerome flattens out the space sled like this *(demonstrate with fold #5)* :

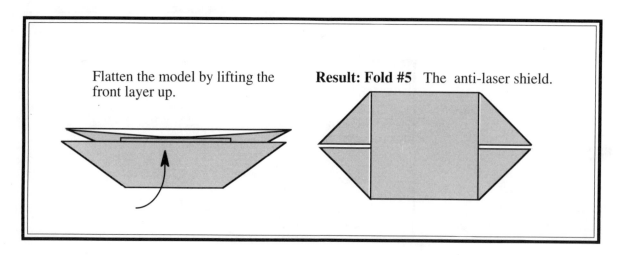

Flatten the model by lifting the front layer up.

**Result: Fold #5** The anti-laser shield.

He makes an anti-laser shield, protecting himself from blasts of incredibly dangerous alien strawberry slush rays. Alien space invaders will not freeze his blood! Suddenly a blast of solar wind flares up and folds two of the corners like this *(demonstrate with fold #6):*

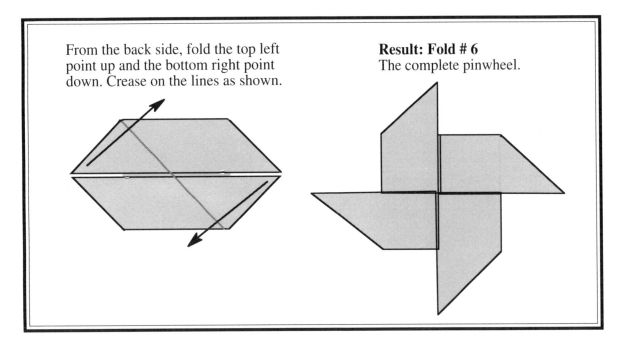

From the back side, fold the top left point up and the bottom right point down. Crease on the lines as shown.

**Result: Fold # 6**
The complete pinwheel.

Jerome jabs his supersonic laser blazer into the middle like this *(insert a pencil into the center and gently blow on the blades)* and up he rises, swept away by the spinning propeller all the way to the top of his space station, all set for more action.

*(Spin the blades as though they were carrying Jerome away).*

"Up, up and away! Commander Jerome B. Cartwright to the rescue!"

# Summary of folding directions:

Fold a square in half to form a center crease. Then fold both sides to the center and crease on the dotted lines.

**Result: Fold #1**
Great double doors.

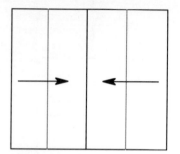

Fold backwards in half through all thicknesses so that the open flaps remain on the surface.

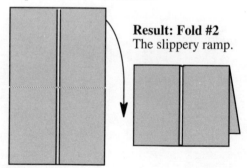

**Result: Fold #2**
The slippery ramp.

Bring the bottom edges up to the top fold on both sides and crease through all thicknesses.

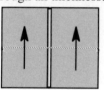

**Result: Fold #3**
The mini space shuttle.

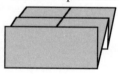

Insert index fingers into both sides of the first layer and pull out to the sides. Flip the entire model over and repeat the procedure for the back layer.

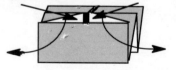

**Result: Fold #4**  The anti-gravitational space sled.

Flatten the model by lifting the front layer up.

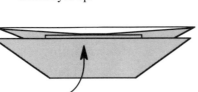

**Result: Fold #5** The anti-laser shield.

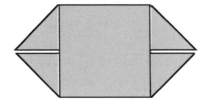

From the back side, fold the top left point up and the bottom right point down. Crease on the lines as shown.

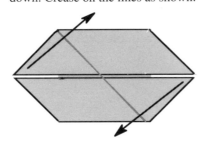

**Result: Fold # 6**
The complete pinwheel.

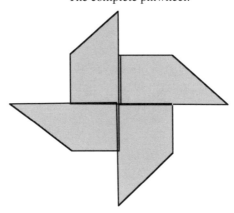

# Optional applications for "To The Rescue"

1. After telling the story, ask the listeners to name the folds leading up to the pinwheel, using the descriptive names from the story, i.e., the tall double doors, the slippery ramp, the space shuttle that wouldn't work, the anti-gravity space sled, and the anti-laser shield *(auditory memory)*. Reconstruct the model, letting the group tell you which step comes next *(visual memory)*. Distribute squares of paper and fold each step together as a group *(synthesis)*.

2. Decorate the finished pinwheel and then completely unfold it to see where the decorative marks are on the original square of paper. Fold it into the final form again and watch the decorations reappear in their intended places *(analysis)*. Before unfolding, ask where the decorative marks will be on the flat paper *(evaluation)*.

3. Experiment with different color and pattern combinations by decorating each pinwheel differently. Blow on the pinwheel and observe how the colors blend together. Evaluate which spinning rates promote the most effective blends.

4. Toss the pinwheels up to let them spin independently to the ground. Analyze the

differences created by dropping them with the blades facing down or the blades facing up. Discuss the applicable aerodynamic principles *(analysis, application)*.

5. Make a group pinwheel collage by inserting pencils or long pins into a large piece of cardboard. Turn on an electric fan to spin all of them simultaneously *(synthesis)*.

6. Attach stems to the pinwheels to form pin-wheel flowers. Make a bulletin board, name tags, or flower pictures *(synthesis)*.

7. What other adventures could Jerome imagine? Write other stories about Jerome and Anthony. Illustrate with other origami folds, models, or clay figures *(synthesis)*.

8. Use this story to introduce or complement discussions or units about:
   a. Sibling relationships.
   b. Saturday morning alternatives.
   c. The joys and pitfalls of pretending.
   d. Snow.
   e. Space. Fantasy vs. reality.
   f. Resourcefulness. Being able to design and create your own diversions.
   g. Responsibility. Was Jerome responsible?
   h. Self-concept. How did Jerome feel?
   i. War, invasions, battles. Feelings about.
   j. Technology. Where did the ideas come from?
   k. Nutrition. Evaluate his breakfast.

| Date | Group | Notes |
|------|-------|-------|
|      |       |       |
|      |       |       |
|      |       |       |
|      |       |       |
|      |       |       |

These sturdy fish are made in only six steps. Folding directions begin on page 82.

**About the story:**

After his best friend moves away, Jerome tries to find a new friend to play with. He is disappointed when he discovers that he's not allowed to have a dog, but he is allowed to have another kind of pet.

**Recommended ages:**

Listening only:  age 3 through adult.
Listening and folding:  age 7 through adult

**Required materials:**

1 square of paper at least 6 inches each side, folded into a fish and then completely unfolded for storytelling.

**Optional introductory statement:**

*I'm going to tell you a story about a boy who feels sad when his best friend moves away. I think you're going to be able to guess who his new friend will be. As I tell you the story, watch carefully as I fold paper into various shapes. This is called origami, or Japanese paper folding. Do you have any questions? (pause) The name of the story is "Jerome's New Friend".*

# Jerome's New Friend

There is something missing in Jerome B. Cartwright's life.

He has a mother who can get stains out of everything, even baseball pants.

He has a father who can build the most amazing inventions from stuff most people throw away.

He has a big brother who used to be fun until he entered Junior High and became tall for his age.

He has a fabulous mind that is always bursting with wonderful schemes and dreams.

But Jerome is missing  a best friend.

Jerome used to have a best friend..........

A  buddy who lived in the same apartment building who could play every day after school.

A pal to go adventuring with.

A partner in daring exploits.

The only person in the world he trusted with his secret code.

Someone who played pretending games without being embarrassed.

A guy his own age whose Mom never ran out of the world's best peanut butter sandwiches.

But then overnight, things changed! One day his best friend lived in the building and the very next day, he moved hundreds of miles away. Writing letters is OK, but it isn't very exciting. Not like before.

The only kids left in the building are babies who drool and whine all the time, or lazy, boring kids with TV's glued to their faces. Big brother Anthony has not one, but two best friends, and about a hundred second best friends. They all meet down at the Fifth Street basketball court every day after school. But they never let Jerome play with them.

"Hey Jerome! Get the basketball!" they yell.

"Fetch the ball, Jerome!"

Finally one day Jerome has had enough, so instead of retrieving the ball for them as usual, he hollers, "Get the ball yourselves! What do you think I am, a dog or something?"

And that's when he thinks of the perfect solution to his problem. A dog! He will get a dog to be his very own best friend.

Jerome hurries to the back bedroom of his family's apartment where his father has a little shop for his wood-working tools. His father never throws anything away because he can turn scraps and junk into wonderful, useful things. Jerome digs through a pile of old wood and discovers a large square that looks like this *(hold up a plain square of paper)*.

Jerome goes right to work building a house for a big lumbering adventurous dog that will become his new best friend. First, he makes a roof like this *(demonstrate with fold #1)* :

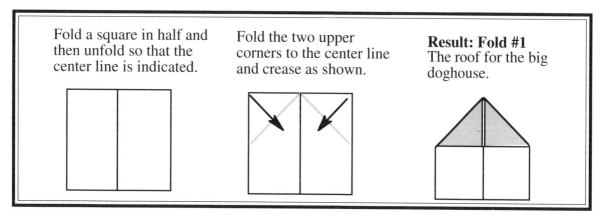

Fold a square in half and then unfold so that the center line is indicated.

Fold the two upper corners to the center line and crease as shown.

**Result: Fold #1**
The roof for the big doghouse.

Next he builds a fancy double door that opens and closes like this *(demonstrate with fold #2 - open and close the door)*:

But before Jerome can finish, his father comes in and says, "I'm sorry Jerome. I know how much you want a new best friend, but it's

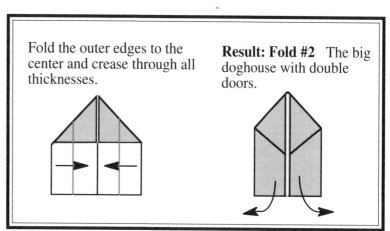

Fold the outer edges to the center and crease through all thicknesses.

**Result: Fold #2** The big doghouse with double doors.

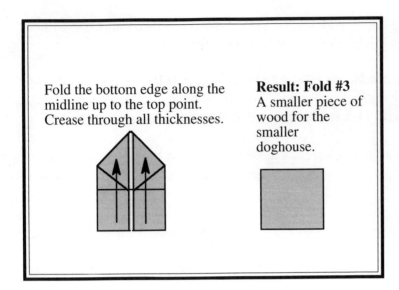

Fold the bottom edge along the midline up to the top point. Crease through all thicknesses.

**Result: Fold #3** A smaller piece of wood for the smaller doghouse.

against the rules to have a big dog in the building. You don't want us to be evicted, do you?"

Jerome doesn't want that to happen, but he isn't ready to give up his plan just yet. If he can't have a big lumbering adventurous dog, then he will settle for a little sly dog, very quick and very smart. Jerome goes right to work building a little house for a little dog. He takes a smaller piece of wood like this (*demonstrate with fold #3*):

Next he builds a roof like this (*Demonstrate with fold #4*):

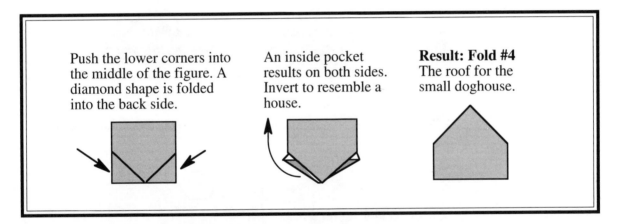

Push the lower corners into the middle of the figure. A diamond shape is folded into the back side.

An inside pocket results on both sides. Invert to resemble a house.

**Result: Fold #4** The roof for the small doghouse.

A little sly dog who is very quick and very smart would want to have two doors, one for going in and one for coming out. So Jerome makes the doors to look like this (*demonstrate with fold #5 by opening and closing the resulting flaps as shown*):

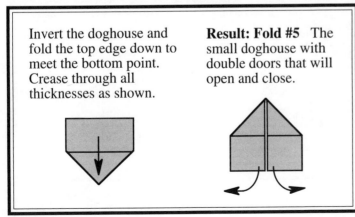

Invert the doghouse and fold the top edge down to meet the bottom point. Crease through all thicknesses as shown.

**Result: Fold #5** The small doghouse with double doors that will open and close.

But before Jerome can finish with his second doghouse, his father comes back in and says a little louder than before:

"I'm sorry, Jerome, but we can't have a big dog or a little dog in this building. No dogs of any kind are allowed. And no cats are allowed, either. No mice. No ferrets. No snakes. No hamsters. No guinea pigs. We can't even have a parakeet. You are just going to have to wait until a new family moves in. I'm sure there will be a new best friend for you any day now."

Jerome is sad about this news. He feels so discouraged that he puts the tools away and sits down and just stares at the pile of old wood, wondering if he and his father can somehow invent a new best friend. Just when he is about to give up, his father calls him out into the living room.

"Jerome, I told you about all the pets we are not allowed to have in the building. But I've just checked the rules again. There is one pet that we can get to be your friend. And we can keep it even after a new family moves in."

Jerome's father takes the small doghouse and folds it like this *(demonstrate with fold #6)*:

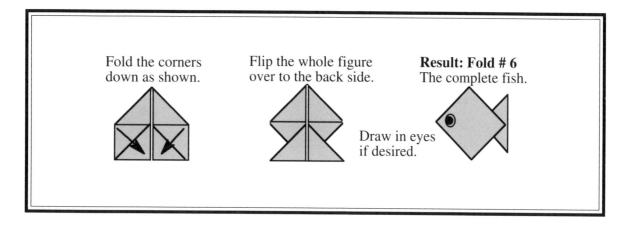

Fold the corners down as shown.

Flip the whole figure over to the back side.

**Result: Fold # 6**
The complete fish.

Draw in eyes
if desired.

"We'll go and get one tomorrow."

Can you guess what Jerome's new friend will be?

# Summary of folding directions:

Fold a square in half and then unfold so that the center line is indicated.

Fold the two upper corners to the center line and crease as shown.

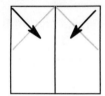

**Result: Fold #1**
The roof for the big doghouse.

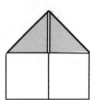

---

Fold the outer edges to the center and crease through all thicknesses.

**Result: Fold #2**
The big doghouse with double doors.

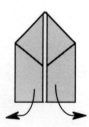

Fold the bottom edge along the midline up to the top point. Crease through all thicknesses.

**Result: Fold #3**
A smaller piece of wood for the smaller doghouse.

---

Push the lower corners into the middle of the figure. A diamond shape is folded into the back side.

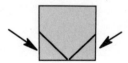

An inside pocket results on both sides. Invert to resemble a house.

**Result: Fold #4**
The roof for the small doghouse.

Invert the doghouse and
fold the top edge down to
meet the bottom point.
Crease through all
thicknesses as shown.

**Result: Fold #5**  The
small doghouse with
double doors that will
open and close.

---

Fold the corners
down as shown.

Flip the whole figure
over to the back side.

**Result: Fold # 6**
The complete fish.

Draw in eyes
if desired.

# Optional applications for "Jerome's New Friend"

1. Review the three steps Jerome followed in constructing both of his dog houses: 1) a square board  2) a roof  3) double doors *(auditory memory)*.  Rebuild the fish, letting the group tell you which step comes next *(visual memory)*.  Distribute squares of paper and construct the fish together as a group *(synthesis)*.  <u>Note</u>: Many beginning folders have trouble with fold #4. It may be helpful to fold those corners up on the outside first so that they will be easier to push inside.

2. Make a "School of Fish" mobile from all of the models. Use different colors and sizes of paper for contrast *(synthesis)*. Emphasize unity and friendship, saying, "We *all* made this together!"

3. Draw scales, fins and eyes onto the completed fish. Unfold to a flat square to see where the drawn features end up. Reconstruct and observe the features come back together *(analysis)*.

4. This is a good story for a group that has a member moving away. After everyone makes a fish, personalize them with names & addresses to present as farewell gifts. Personal notes can also be tucked inside the fish or written on the square of paper before folding.

5. Insert wrapped candy, a small toy or holiday stickers inside the fish. Attach a large metal paper clip and throw them into a "fish pond". Catch the fish with a large magnet attached to string and a fishing rod. This is a fun way to distribute party favors, prizes or special treats.

6. Punch holes in the fish and lace with yarn to make necklaces, earrings, bracelets or ornaments.

7. Use this story to introduce or complement discussions or units about:
   a. Friendship. What makes a friend special?
   b. Sibling relationships.
   c. Pets and pet care.
   d. Moving.
   e. Inventiveness. Forming and testing ideas. The importance of persistence.
   f. Homes. Differences and similarities.
   g. Rules. Are rules fair? Are rules necessary?
   h. Loneliness.
   i. Disappointment.
   j. Making new friends. How to reach out.

| Date | Group | Notes |
|------|-------|-------|
|  |  |  |
|  |  |  |
|  |  |  |
|  |  |  |
|  |  |  |

# For more information....

## National Organizations

The following groups provide members with informative newsletters, sponsor annual conventions, special events and festivals, and compile complete lists of regional groups, materials, and resources. Membership is inexpensive and easily obtained by inquiring at the addresses listed below.

National Association for the Preservation and Perpetuation of Storytelling (NAPPS), P. O. Box 309, Jonesborough, TN 37659. Phone 615-753-2171.

The Friends of The Origami Center of America, 15 West 77 St., New York, NY 10024-5192. Phone 212-769-5635.

## Other sources for material containing both paper folding and text:

Gross, Gay Merrill, 1991, *World of Crafts: Folding Napkins*, p. 117, New York, NY: Mallard Press.

Pellowski, Anne, 1987, *Family Storytelling Handbook,* p. 74-84 ( two stories written by Gay Merrill Gross), New York, NY: Macmillan Publishing Co.

Rey, H. A., 1952, *Curious George Rides A Bike*, New York, NY: Houghton.

Schimmel, Nancy, 1982, *Just Enough To Make A Story: A Sourcebook For Storytellers,* p. 20-32, Berkeley, CA: Sisters' Choice Press.

## Books for beginning paper folders:

Adair, Ian, 1975, *Papercrafts: Step by Step Series*, London: David & Charles Publishers.

Ayture-Scheele, Zulal, 1987, *The Great Origami Book,* New York, NY: Sterling Publishing Co.

Ayture-Scheele, Zulal, 1986, *Origami In Color: paperfolding fun,* New York, NY: Gallery Books.

Kobayashi, Kazuo and Yamaguchi, Makoto, 1987, *Origami for Parties*, New York: Kodansha International.

Lewis, Shari and Oppenheimer, Lillian, 1962, *Folding Paper Puppets,* New York, NY: Stein and Day Publishers

Lewis, Shari and Oppenheimer, Lillian, 1965, *Folding Paper Masks,* New York, NY: Dutton.

Randlett, Samuel, 1961, *The Best of Origami*, New York: E. P. Dutton & Co., Inc.

Sarasas, Claude, 1964, *The ABC's Of Origami*, Rutland, VT: Charles E. Tuttle, Inc.

Takahama, Toshie, 1985, *The Joy of Origami*, Tokyo, Japan: Shufunotomo/Japan Publications. (also by the same author: *Origami Toys, Origami for Fun, Quick and Easy Origami*).

Weiss, Stephen, 1984, *Wings & Things: origami that flies*, New York, NY: St. Martin's Press.

## Books with historic information about origami:

Honda, Isao, 1965, *The World of Origami*, Rutland, VT: Japan Publications Trading Co.

Lang, Robert J., 1988, *The Complete Book of Origami*, New York, NY: Dover Publications, Inc.

Randlett, Samuel, 1961, *The Art of Origami*, New York, NY: E. P. Dutton & Co., Inc.

## Books relating to storytelling techniques:

Greene, Ellin, *Storytelling: Art and Technique*, New York, NY: R. R. Bowker Co.

Herman, Gail, *Storytelling: A Triad in the Arts*, Mansfield Center, CT: Creative Learning Press.

Livo, Norma, *Storytelling: Process and Practice*, Englewood, CO: Libraries Unlimited.

Pellowski, Anne, 1987, *Family Storytelling Handbook*, New York, NY: Macmillan Publishing Co.

Schimmel, Nancy, 1982, *Just Enough To Make a Story: A Sourcebook For Storytelling*, Berkeley, CA: Sisters' Choice.

Christine Petrell Kallevig is available as a keynote speaker or to present Storigami demonstrations at conventions, workshops, assemblies, or festivals. Contact the publisher, Storytime Ink International, P. O. Box 813, Newburgh, IN 47629 for details.

# Glossary

**Activity Therapy:** A general category that usually encompasses music therapy, art therapy, dance therapy, recreational therapy, and occupational therapy. These therapies are generally found in psychiatric, rehabilitation, nursing, or educational centers.

**Analysis:** A thinking skill related to the ability to reason, decipher consequences, or determine procedural steps or components.

**Auditory memory:** Thoughts, information, or experiences derived through hearing or listening.

**Bloom's Taxonomy:** A system developed by Benjamin S. Bloom *(Taxonomy of Educational Objectives, Handbook I:Cognitive Domain, New York: David McKay Co., Inc., 1956)* that organizes educational objectives into two basic realms, cognitive and affective. The cognitive hierarchy starts with knowledge and then progresses to comprehension, application, analysis, synthesis and evaluation. The higher order thought processes (analysis, synthesis, and evaluation) are of major concern when promoting children's abilities to function as independent, effective thinkers.

**Evaluation:** A thinking skill related to the ability to make judgements, make decisions, or set criteria based on a combination of observed data and probable consequences.

**Fine motor coordination:** The ability to integrate information derived from the senses (sight, sound, tactile) with small motions of the fingers and hands. Folding origami is an example.

**Folklore:** Traditions, beliefs, stories, and art forms preserved by a culture's common people, often using oral teaching techniques within the family social structure. Origami and storytelling are both examples.

**Gami** *(kami):* A Japanese word meaning paper.

**Irony:** A literary technique where the outcome is different or opposite from what may be expected.

**Kinesthetic memory:** Thoughts, information, or experiences derived through actions or tactile sensations.

**Left brain:** Refers to the left lobe of the cerebral cortex, generally considered to be the site of analysis, word processing, and linear and sequential thought processes. Understanding a sequence of story events is an example.

**Literal interpretation:** Understanding a story based solely on its plot and characters, without considering the author's point of view.

**Mountain folding:** A basic origami folding technique which results in a tent-like or mountain shaped fold, as in fold #1 on page 36.

**Ori:** A Japanese word meaning folded.

**Origami:** Paper folding techniques preserved and developed through Japanese folklore, generally involving the folding of paper into two or three dimensional figures without cutting and gluing. It has now spread throughout the world and includes thousands of creative and traditional models. *Origami* also refers to the folded figure itself, i.e., the folded rabbit is an origami.

**Right brain:** Refers to the right lobe of the cerebral cortex, generally considered to be the site of emotions, artistic talent, intuition, and abstract, holistic thought processes. Imagining the shape of the final origami figure is an example.

**Storigami:** A term coined by Christine Petrell Kallevig (*Folding Stories: Storytelling and Origami Together As One, Storytime Ink Intl., Newburgh, IN, 1991*) to describe the concept of combining storytelling and origami by illustrating stories with progressive origami folds.

**Symbolic interpretation:** Relating characters, events, or settings to other personal, social, or political entities, based either on an author's or reader's personal points of view.

**Synthesis:** A thinking skill related to creating, designing, or composing new thoughts or objects.

**Valley folding:** A basic origami technique resulting in a valley shaped fold, as in fold #3 on page 61.

**Visual memory:** Thoughts, information, or experiences derived through seeing or watching.

**Whole brain:** Refers to learning techniques which utilize both the right and left hemispheres of the cerebral cortex, resulting in greater memory retention and more rapid learning.

# Index

## Other items available from

## INTERNATIONAL

*Holiday Folding Stories: Storytelling and Origami Together For Holiday Fun*

by Christine Petrell Kallevig

Nine original stories illustrated by nine easy origami models, for ages five through adult. The stories are based on Columbus Day, Halloween, Thanksgiving, Christmas, Hanukkah, Valentine's Day, Easter, May Day, and Mother's Day. Includes dozens of suggestions for optional activities and party ideas. ISBN 0-9628769-1-7

*Pre-folded origami models, complete with instructions and Japanese origami paper.*

The origami models featured in **Folding Stories** and **Holiday Folding Stories** are pre-folded in richly colored origami paper. Package includes an instruction booklet and 36 sheets of origami paper in assorted colors and sizes.